The Origami Bible

The Origami Bible

Nick Robinson

With a short history by David Lister

NORTH LIGHT BOOKS

First published in 2004 by

Collins & Brown Limited

The Chrysalis Building

Bramley Road

London, W10 6SP

An imprint of **Chrysalis** Books Group plc

Distributed to the trade markets in North America by
North Light books, an imprint of F&W Publications, Inc.
4700 East Galbraith road, Cincinnati, OH 45236
(800) 289 0963

ISBN: 1-58180-517-9

Designed by Roger Hammond
Edited by Hilary Mandelberg
Illustrations by Nick Robinson
Photography by Neil Sutherland

9 8 7 6 5 4 3 2 1

Color reproduction by Classicscan, Singapore
Printed by Kyodo Printing Co Limited, Singapore

Contents

Foreword

The miracles held within a simple square of paper soon become apparent when you begin to fold it. Edges neatly match up with creases as the paper dances a sort of careless, yet perfect ballet. Patterns of folds, seemingly stolen from a Moorish palace, enable the paper to collapse elegantly into a new geometric shape, a recognizable animal, a neat container, or a simple toy that performs an unexpected movement.

Nick Robinson preaches the gospel of this new world of origami, aided by this collection of his own designs and a few by other notable folders. The generosity and friendship of origami enthusiasts everywhere demonstrate that this is a universal language and tell us that the world of paper folding is remarkably small. At the same time, emerging ideas and concepts show us that origami is boundless. The limitations imposed by the square that is neither to be cut, nor decorated nor glued, merely folded, often mean that the creator overcomes apparently insuperable problems with elegant and economic solutions. Restriction stimulates richness.

If you find that you have been converted by origami, make a point of joining one of the many organizations devoted to the spread of its knowledge everywhere. Exchanging ideas with others who share this passion will expand your skill and knowledge rapidly, and is the best way to learn and progress.

I wish you good luck on your origami pilgrimage!

Dave Brill
CHAIRMAN OF THE BRITISH ORIGAMI SOCIETY

Introduction

Origami is a Japanese word meaning "paper folding." For many years essentially a traditional artform, paper folding has seen an unprecedented growth in both the diversity of subject matter and the range of techniques available to the creative folder. This book presents a wide range of stimulating and previously unpublished designs, carefully chosen to illustrate both techniques and concepts in origami.

The intention of this book, however, is to offer more than just another selection of designs. I'd like readers to feel they can create their own designs and I've included tips and hints with many of the designs so that you can explore the fun of creating origami as well as folding it. I firmly believe that everyone is born with a talent and that given the right environment, it will emerge. It may be that your talent isn't in creating origami, but it's fun to try!

I'd also like to share with you the fun that you can have as part of the worldwide origami community. There are thousands of folders around the world who are happy to exchange diagrams and folds with you. This might be through the Internet or by more traditional means. I have made many, many good friends through origami and their friendship is every bit as important as the origami we fold.

A Short History of Paper Folding by David Lister

TODAY THE WORD *origami* is an accepted part of English and of many other languages. It is the Japanese word for "paper folding," but paper is not the only material to have been folded. Cloth and leather are obvious alternatives. Despite its stiffness, it is even possible to fold papyrus and the earliest example of "paper" folding we have is of an Egyptian map, probably dating from Hellenistic times and now in a museum in Milan. It shows a Nubian gold mine and is folded just like a modern road map. Even so, the material that is pre-eminently suitable for folding is paper. We cannot precisely date when paper was first folded, but we can, at least, be sure that it could not have happened before paper became freely available in different countries.

It is popularly assumed that the Japanese "invented" paper folding, but despite many confident assertions, nobody can be sure. In fact, the first people to fold paper may well have been the Chinese. Paper was invented in China, and good paper suitable for writing, and presumably for folding, was being made by AD 100.

Knowledge of paper making was taken with Buddhism from China to Korea and from there to Japan, where it arrived around AD 550.

The Arabs learned how to make paper from Chinese prisoners they took in Samarkand in Central Asia in AD 751. By 1036 papermaking reached Cordoba in Moorish Spain. It reached France in 1189, Germany in 1388, and England in 1490.

Despite this, however, we do not have any firm evidence of recreational paper folding in Europe before 1600. Perhaps surprisingly, the same applies to Japan, where the first evidence of recreational paper folding, as opposed to ceremonial paper folding, does not appear until after 1600.

Was the skill discovered in one country and spread from there, or was it discovered independently in different places? It is usually assumed that paper folding was first practiced in the East, either in China or Japan, and that it was taken from there along the land or sea routes to Europe, but it is equally possible that it was discovered independently in Europe. Or, unlikely as it may seem, it may be that it was first discovered in the West and taken to the East. There is no evidence one way or the other.

The Japanese tradition

We have no more than a few scattered glimpses of early paper folding in Japan, where paper was used in many ways, utilitarian, religious, and ceremonial. During the Heian period (AD 794–1185) the cultivated classes took pleasure in letter writing and it was considered discourteous to send a letter unless it was folded in a precise manner. A cultured man would usually carry a *tato*, which was a simply folded paper wallet to hold handkerchiefs or papers for writing. In this period paper was also used as a material for wrapping medicines and spices, with the wrappers becoming rather formalized in style.

Formalization was always a tendency in Japan, and in the Muromachi period (1333–1600), society became governed by rigid codes of etiquette regulated by schools of behavior, such as the

Ogasawara School. In particular, the giving of presents was closely circumscribed, etiquette demanding that every gift, especially of flowers, should have its own special kind of paper wrapper. These wrappers, known as *tsutsumi*, were elaborately pleated fan shapes. The use of *tsutsumi* continued throughout the Edo period (1600–1868) and even today, although their use has declined rapidly in modern Japan, they are still used to wrap the gifts that are sometimes exchanged by Japanese families at formal betrothal ceremonies.

One surprising formal gift, which would be given on an auspicious occasion, was of abalone. This was the stretched flesh of a shellfish known as *noshi awabi*. The wrapper was called a noshi tsutsumi. Later, the abalone was replaced by a symbolic strip of yellow paper, and the *noshi tsutsumi* itself became a mere symbol, with its name shortened to *noshi*. Miniature *noshi* are still customarily attached to gifts in Japan today, much as, in the West, we might attach a gift tag.

Another use of paper in Japan was in the zigzagged paper streamers known as *O-Sheda* and *Gohei* which still decorate Shinto shrines and other sacred places. They are made by a cut-and-fold technique. *O-Sheda* usually hang from a *shimenaw* or sacred rope marking the boundary of the sacred place. They were probably derived from strips of cloth and it is most likely that they originated in the Heian period. A *Gohei* is a smaller, double zigzag streamer attached to a short rod. It stands in a shrine, large or small, where it denotes the presence of the deity honored there.

Another early ceremonial use of paper was very different. It was used to protect the mouth of flasks containing rice wine or sake. The paper was smoothed down around the neck of the flask and tied with a cord. The smoothing down made a series of creases radiating from the center of the

paper and it has been suggested that the discarded covers were fancifully thought to resemble butterflies. The paper covers were then formalized and it became customary to decorate flasks and other containers used for sake with pairs of folded paper butterflies, known as *Ocho* (male) and *Mecho* (female) butterflies.

At a traditional Japanese wedding sake is sipped by the bride and groom to seal the contract and the *Mecho* and *Ocho* butterflies are still associated with weddings today. They are the nearest kind of ancient Japanese paper folding we can find to modern recreational folding and we can see glimpses in the butterflies of modern origami models folded from the Waterbomb base (see page 30). Japanese commentators find it difficult to put a date on the origin of the butterflies. Some suggest the Muromachi period, but they may date from the Heian period. Whatever the date, we know that the butterflies have been folded for many centuries.

Although paper folding for play or recreation may have begun to evolve earlier, it is only in the Edo period that we begin to find any information about it. In the 17th century, the first illustrations of recreational folds begin to appear and some of them occasionally appear in the decoration of the flowing robes of the wealthier classes of the time. We find such familiar folds as the Chinese junk, the classic crane, simple boats and the wandering flute player, known as Komoso. All these folds are fairly simple and are of the kind that are usually associated with children. In fact, however, the illustrations we have usually show them being folded by young ladies from the wealthier classes. It is not until the 19th century that pictures of children folding become frequent.

We have many Japanese prints and woodcuts illustrating folded figures from the 17th and 18th centuries. One important woodcut of 1734 shows

Komoso with the same type of boats and cranes are seen on the robes of the earlier Edo period. This woodcut also shows a cubic box, which was apparently the first modular model and a *sanbo*, or container on legs that is still folded today. The conclusion is that origami for play was well established by the 18th century.

In 1797, we have our first glimpse of a new, more complicated kind of folding, which was clearly the work of adults and not intended for children. The year 1797 saw the publication of *Senbazuru Orikata*, a book with instructions for folding the classic crane, not singly but in groups, as well as chains of cranes linked together. The initial square, cut from very strong white paper, is cut into a series of smaller squares joined at the corners. Some of the models are simple, with no more than two or three cranes, while others consist of a hundred or more linked cranes.

Senbazuru Orikata originated from the Choen Ji Temple in what is now the Mia prefecture. Also from the same source and dated 1797 are two printed sheets known as the *Chushingura Orikata*. One shows illustrations from the famous Japanese play, *Chushingura*; the other has diagrams for folding the characters of the play. A note on one of the sheets announces that there will be other publications in the same series, but so far none has come to light.

Nevertheless, we know that this kind of "adult" paper folding was quite extensively practiced in

the 19th century. The *Kayaragusa* or *Kan no mado*, a hand-written encyclopedia in 283 slender volumes, dates from 1845. Volumes 27 and 28 are devoted to paper folding. Its models include the *Ocho* and *Mecho* butterflies as well as formal *tsutsumi* wrappers for spices and several kinds of flowers. In addition, there are instructions for folding the characteristic sitting human figures of the kind still folded for the traditional display of dolls on Girls' Day in Japan.

By contrast with these, the rest of the folds illustrated are complex recreational folds of animals, insects, and a magnificent crab, several of them beginning with a deeply cut, six-pointed star base. The splendid dragonfly became especially famous. It seems that these folds may have come from the same source as the *Senbazuru Orikata*, perhaps from one of the promised, and as yet undiscovered, books. When the *Kayragusa* came to light in the mid-1960s, Kosho Uchiyama, the youngest of a family of distinguished folders, recalled that his grandmother had folded models in just this style. Sadly, all of them had been destroyed in an earthquake and during bombing in the Second World War. Other evidence of similar advanced folding has come to light, so we can be confident that as well as the simpler "children's" folding, there was also a more complex style of folding that was practiced by adults.

It has been suggested that paper folding for "play" was passed down from mother to daughter as practice for more serious formal folding. This approach to paper folding was changed by the introduction

RIGHT: *"Happy Origami" from 1960 by Tatsuo Miyawaki, part of a series to teach the basics of origami.*

吉沢 章 創作おりがみ集

たのしい おりがみ

鎌倉書房

LEFT: *An early work by the Japanes Master, Akira Yoshizawa.*

into Japan of kindergartens by the followers of Friedrich Fröbel in around 1880. Already an invariable feature of the Fröbel kindergartens in Europe, paper folding was brought to Japan by the Fröbel teachers. It reminded the Japanese of their own paper folding and a cross-fertilization between the two traditions resulted. Paper folding was then introduced into the more traditional Japanese schools and the folding that had formerly been passed down in families became a school activity.

Books about children's folding began to be published in Japan about 1890, and the word *origami*, which had hitherto been occasionally used for formal paper folding, was applied to children's folding for the first time. As a result, recreational paper folding underwent a general revival in Japan.

The traditional children's models began to be collected together and preserved. Two collectors during the 1930s and 1940s were Isao Honda and Florence Sakade. In the 1950s, they were inspired to make the traditional Japanese folds available to the West in a series of books in European languages. However, the origami scene changed dramatically with the rising of a new star of Japanese origami, the most famous paper-folder of all time, Akira Yoshizawa.

The Western tradition

We must now go back in time and trace the early history of paper folding in Europe. Apart from the Egyptian map, already mentioned, the earliest records of folding in Europe are in the frequent pictures that have come down to us from Egypt, Greece, Rome, and Byzantium which show that pleating was, from the earliest times, a popular way of decorating clothing.

While pleated clothing may seem remote from paper folding, the folding of dinner napkins is considered to be closely related. The vogue for folding napkins began in the 16th century, when princely tables came to be decorated with napkins folded in the form of fruits, animals, birds, and sailing ships. Illustrations of these have survived in books written in Italy in 1629 and Germany in 1657. Most of the creations are made from large, starched napkins that have been pleated and cross-pleated so that the resulting double-pleated cloth can be molded into the chosen fantasies. It seems a long way from modern origami, but the Italian and German books also illustrate a few simple individual napkin folds. Significantly, both illustrate the folds that are still familiar to us today and is known as the Waterbomb base and the Blintz base.

Anyone who holds a piece of paper instinctively plays with it. Folding the sides or the corners together is one obvious thing to do. Combine both the diagonal creases and the horizontal creases and it is easy to arrive at what we know as the Preliminary base and its close relative, the Waterbomb base. These are two of today's most significant starting folds or bases. Another way of playing with a paper square is by folding the four corners to the center. This can be repeated a second and even a third time in the technique known as "blintzing" the square. One of the models folded in this way from a square napkin is the Waterlily. Neither the Italian nor the German book refers to the Waterlily, but it is mentioned in a book on culinary arts dated 1682 by an Englishman, Giles Rose. He called it a Cross.

The "double blintzing" technique is also used to form the Windmill base which is another fundamental base of paper folding and may be behind what is sometimes called the "Astrological Square," a pattern used for several centuries for preparing horoscopes. The Astrological Square was first devised by Gerado Cremone, an Italian who lived in Toledo in the 12th century. It seems inexplicable today that a square design should be used for representing the positions of heavenly bodies and their rotary motion, yet this kind of horoscope persisted in Europe until the mid-19th century.

A later use of the Double Blintz suggests that the Astrological Square may originally have been folded. In the 16th century, there was a tradition in central Europe of preparing "paten-brieves" or baptismal certificates, which were given by godparents to babies on their baptism. Inscribed with pious pictures, messages, and the date of the baptism, they were folded into a Double Blintz. The folded paten-brief of Friedrich Fröbel is still exhibited in the Fröbel Museum at Bad Blankenberg in Germany. It has been conjectured that during the Reformation, as astrology fell into disfavor with the Church, baptismal brieves were used instead of similarly folded horoscopes, which may have been drawn up for the birth of a child during the Middle Ages.

In Europe, only a few traditional folds used bases with a radial crease pattern, such as the Preliminary and Waterbomb bases, and neither the radial Bird base nor the Frog base was known. The Inflated Waterbomb is also known as a Fly Trap. It is mentioned in 1614 in John Webster's play, *The Duchess of Malfi,* in which Webster refers to the paper prisons in which small boys trap flies. The same model is known today in Egypt, China, and Japan. Other models related to the Waterbomb are the Kettle and the Bellows, while the familiar Swallow or Glider also begins with the Waterbomb base.

Much more common than the Waterbomb base is the Windmill base related to the Blintz. With a little adaptation, many models can be made from it, not least the Windmill itself. Robert Harbin (see page 17) called the Windmill Base the Multiform.

One of the best-known European folds is the curious angular bird resembling a tangram figure. It is generally known by its Spanish name of *Pajarita,* but in France is known as *Cocotte,* while in Japan it is known as *Inu* or dog. Despite intensive research, it is not known when or where the *Pajarita* originated, although the Spanish tenaciously claim it as their own.

Models folded from the Double Blintz or Multiform are common in 19th-century Europe. Friedrich Fröbel recollected how, as a child, he folded the Miner, a two-piece figure sometimes known as the Suit of Clothes. The simple but strong box known in Japan as a *Masu* box, is also a Multiform fold. Dating from 1806 we have a Dutch print, which has a picture of the more complicated Chinese junk. The junk too, is a fold of the Multiform family. It is possible that it came to the Netherlands from the East by the eastern trade routes, but we are not sure.

Other important early European folds closely related to the *Pajarita* are the German foot soldiers and mounted soldiers with their horses, which date from between 1810 and 1820. These are today exhibited in museums in Dresden and Nuremberg and show how sophisticated paper folding could be at that time.

Throughout the 19th century, references to paper folding in Europe become very frequent. As has already been stated, Fröbel adopted paper folding in his system of child education, first as a way for children to discover geometry. He used the traditional folds to guide children toward mathematical folding. Then he perceived that paper folding could be a creative activity and he then encouraged the folding of paper patterns from squares of paper by first "blintzing" them. Fröbel died in 1852, but his successors continued to teach paper folding and their many books show how extensive was the repertoire of traditional models known in Europe in the 19th century.

Until 1854, Japan remained a closed and isolated country. As a result of the gunboat diplomacy of Commodore Matthew Perry in that year, Japan opened her borders to the West. Among the many exchanges that followed, Japanese magicians began to tour Europe and the United States. It is recounted how, in the 1870s, they would astonish their audiences by producing a large square of paper. With a few deft flips, the magician had a bird flapping in his hands. The secret was that the square had been pre-creased, but in the glare of the limelight this was not evident. The introduction of the Flapping Bird transformed Western folding. It was first

published in the *Boy's Own Paper* in June 1886 and it soon made frequent appearances in European books of parlor science and children's recreations. The Jumping Frog soon followed and with these two folds the Bird base and the Frog base were introduced to the West.

Toward the end of the 19th century, interest in paper folding was invigorated by Miguel de Unamuno, the Spanish philosopher and poet who was the rector of Salamanca University until his death at the end of 1936. He delighted in the playfulness of paper folding and when he wrote his novel *Amor y Pedagogía* in 1902, he appended to it his "Jottings for a Treatise on Cocottology." This was a mock-serious treatise on the *Pajarita* in which he poked fun at the pseudo-scientific treatises common at that time. In the same year, he wrote a short article about paper folding for the Argentinian journal, *Caras y Caretas*. This article was illustrated with a somewhat angular standing bird, which he had created using the Bird base, which he may have derived from the Japanese conjurors. Unamuno's bird also made use of the "Sideways Turn," which was later to be used independently and to even greater effect by Akira Yoshizawa in Japan.

Unamuno's fresh approach inspired a lively interest in paper folding among the students of the University of Salamanca and it spread to the rest of Spain during the first half of the 20th century. A few, led by Dr. Vicente Solorzano Sagredo, brought the new ideas to Argentina where they took root and where a new group of paper-folders flourished. Among the new

RIGHT: *Paper model making for day and Sunday schools from 1915.*

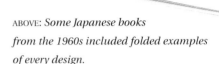

Argentinian folders was Ligia Montoya, who had been a student in Salamanca and who developed her own delicate style. Another was Adolfo Cerceda, a variety performer, who left Argentina to travel the world with his knife-throwing act. He later became one of the folders associated with the Origami Center in New York.

Meanwhile, in northern Europe and North America, conjurors continued to use paper folding. In Britain Will Blythe wrote two books of *Paper Magic* in 1920 and 1923, both of them consisting half of paper folding and half of magic with paper. In 1922, Houdini wrote a book, also named *Paper Magic*. The book includes the Flapping Bird and a few other folds. Two other American magicians, William D. Murray and Francis J. Rigney, wrote *Fun with Paper Folding* in 1928. Apart from the Fröbelian books, this was the first monograph on paper folding in English. In 1937 another book devoted to paper folding but with a few other paper plays, *Paper Toy Making*, was written by Margaret Campbell, a South African grandmother. Mrs. Campbell had traveled in the East and she introduced a new collection of traditional Japanese folds to the West.

Conjurors also took part in the craze for folding dollar bills, which was mainly a diversion in bars, where bartenders would use it to entertain customers. In the mid-1930s it was reported that at a magicians' convention in Chicago, all the people there were wearing a finger ring folded from a dollar bill. Bill folding was popular among the armed forces during the Second World War, following which the first booklets about it began to appear. In the 1960s money folding was absorbed into the rising origami movement.

ABOVE: *Some Japanese books from the 1960s included folded examples of every design.*

The origami revolution

During the decade of the 1950s paper folding was completely transformed. From being an unsystematic collection of traditional folds, it was changed into a coherent activity with rules, terminology, and techniques of its own.

The transformation began in 1945 when an American, Gershon Legman, broke his leg and rediscovered his childhood pastime of paper folding during a period of enforced inactivity. He researched the subject in major American libraries and began communicating with everybody he could find who shared his interest. He also sought out paper folders in Japan and South America whose names he had come across.

However, the signal for dramatic change came in Japan with the publication of the picture magazine *Asahi Graf* in January 1952. To mark the new year it illustrated 12 origami designs for the figures of the Japanese zodiac by the previously unknown Akira Yoshizawa. Yoshizawa was born in 1911 and had developed his skills from childhood unaided. He discovered new techniques of folding, but in addition he had an innate genius for seemingly bringing his models to life. One aspect of his art was that he stressed the importance of creating new models instead of slavishly copying traditional ones. He continued to practice his art during the

Second World War while working as a medical orderly in the Japanese army and after the war, struggled to make paper folding his living, eking out his income by doing menial jobs. Slowly he came to the notice of a group of teachers and showed his art at their conferences. His work was then discovered by Tradasu Iizawa, the editor of *Asahi Graf*. Enthusiastic recognition by the Japanese public followed; an exhibition in central Tokyo came next, and Yoshizawa's life was transformed.

Then something unexpected happened. A Japanese publisher brought Yoshizawa to the notice of Gershon Legman, who by had then moved to France. In 1953, after some difficulty, Legman managed to get in touch with Yoshizawa who sent the American models he had folded for his exhibition in Tokyo. In the autumn of 1955 Legman

was then able to put on an exhibition of Yoshizawa's work at the Stedjlik Museum in Amsterdam. The exhibition was an immediate success and it brought Yoshizawa to the notice of the Western world only three years after he had been recognized in Japan.

In 1953 in Britain, another stage magician, Robert Harbin, became keenly interested in paper folding after coming across Margaret Campbell's *Paper Toy Making* and he started collecting every scrap of information on the subject he could find. By a remarkable stroke of fortune he was put in touch with Gershon Legman and they immediately exchanged everything they knew about the subject. In particular, Legman told Harbin about Yoshizawa's wonderful folding.

Robert Harbin was influential in the entertainment world and by 1955, he was demonstrating paper folding on BBC children's television. In 1956 he published his own book called *Paper Magic*, in which he summarized everything so far known about the art. Harbin also identified the common basic folds and techniques and gave colorful names to its most important moves, such as Petal Folds and Rabbit's Ears. Harbin also emphasized the importance of Yoshizawa's ideas of creative paper folding. None of Yoshizawa's models was included in the book, but it referred to Yoshizawa as being "far and away the greatest folder in the world and devoted to this delicate and graceful artform to an extent which it is hardly possible to believe."

In 1957, Yoshizawa published his own book, *Origami Dokuhon 1*. In it he not only

BELOW: *Enthusiasts travel around the world to attend the annual origami conventions. A good time is had by all!*

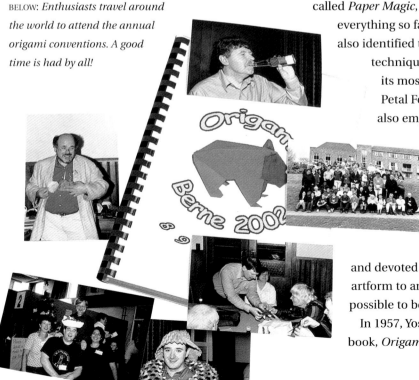

presented many of his models, but he also introduced his system of notation using arrows and dotted lines for mountain and valley folds. Although the book was in Japanese, the clear notation could be understood by everyone and enthusiasm for Yoshizawa's new origami spread .

Meanwhile, in New York around 1929, during tedious visits to the doctor, a mother called Lillian Oppenheimer had entertained her sick daughter, Molly, with the help of Murray and Rigney's book (see page 16). This book contains the *Flapping Bird* but after Molly got better, Lillian forgot all about paper folding. Her interest was reawakened about 1953 when she saw a distant relative folding the *Flapping Bird* at a party. She eagerly sought out how to fold the little bird and with her friend Frieda Lourie she enthusiastically began to teach and promote the traditional models to anyone who would listen. In 1957 Lillian was sent a copy of Robert Harbin's *Paper Magic* and she received it with enthusiasm. This was paper folding such as she had never imagined! Her evangelistic zeal was redoubled and she immediately crossed the Atlantic to meet Robert Harbin. She missed meeting Gershon Legman in France only because he was away from home.

At the same time, Lillian decided that the term "paper folding" was not distinctive enough and she began to use the Japanese word "origami" instead. This unusual word quickly captured the imagination of folders and it became established in the English language from 1958. In May 1958 Lillian was featured in an article in the *New York Times* and as a direct result of this she appeared on one television program after another. Origami was suddenly famous!

Lillian Oppenheimer was not content to rest on her laurels. She organized origami-teaching sessions at the Japan Center in New York and also wrote a newsletter, named *The Origamian,* for folders who could not get there. Thus the Origami Center, really just an extension of Lillian Oppenheimer, came into being. For the first time, origami had its own center of activity and became a focus for folders not only in the United States but in other countries, too. Lillian later also made origami books available, including those of Yoshizawa, and organized meetings of folders in her own home. In March 1959, she visited Akira Yoshizawa in Tokyo and the following May she contributed a display of origami, including many of Yoshizawa's creations, to the exhibition, "Plane Geometry and Fancy Figures," held at the Cooper Union Museum (now the Cooper-Hewitt Museum) in New York.

As a result of the separate, but linked initiatives by Akira Yoshizawa, Gershon Legman, Robert Harbin and Lillian Oppenheimer, origami was transformed into a dynamic recreation, even an art form. People who had previously enjoyed paper folding in isolation now communicated with each other and discovered the new ideas of Yoshizawa. Existing folders, such as Jack Skillman, Robert Neal, and George Rhoads, were drawn in, as well as Ligia Montoya in Argentina and Adolfo Cerceda, now living in the United States. In the days before the Internet, an astonishingly lively exchange by correspondance took place between them all. New geniuses such as Fred Rohm and Neal Elias quickly emerged and in 1961, another new folder, Samuel Randlett, wrote a book, *The Art of Origami*, which built on the work of Yoshizawa and Harbin rationalized the system of folding techniques and bases. In 1964, Randlett wrote *The Best of Origami,* while Robert Harbin wrote *Secrets of Origami*. These three books presented the work of the leading new Western folders to a worldwide audience. Together, they summarized what had passed while becoming a springboard for the future.

The Origami Center was the creation of Lillian Oppenheimer and had no formal membership or organization. To be Lillian's friend was to automatically to be a member. She gathered around her many paper-folders, some of whom gave her considerable help. Among these were Alice Gray, an entomologist at the American Museum of Natural History in New York, who edited *The Origamian* for many years. Another helper was Michael Shall, who had come to New York as a young teacher. He became convinced that as Lillian became older, a more formal organization would be needed. So Michael, with the support of Alice Gray, proposed a parallel organization to assist the Origami Center. In April 1981 the loose group of associates of the Origami Center was formally organized as a not-for-profit limited company with the name, Friends of the Origami Center. When Alice Gray retired, arrangements were made for the Friends to continue to use her office at the Museum of Natural History and one by one, the Friends took over the functions of the Origami Center.

When Lillian died on July 24, 1992, the Origami Center died with her and the Friends' name was changed to "Origami USA." They continue to have an office in the Museum of Natural History and remain the main origami society in the United States, linked to many smaller regional groups there as well as to an ever-increasing number of origami societies all around the world.

The enrichment of Origami

In Japan a new generation of Japanese folders emerged, including Kosho Uchiyama and Yoyoaki Kawai, two older folders and Kunihiko Kasahara, a younger man. By the early 1950s information about the Japanese folders began to filter to the West.

ABOVE: *Two of the seminal English books devoted to paperfolding.*

In the summer of 1965, Toyaki Kawai led a party of Japanese folders to New York to visit the New York World Fair. Among them was Mrs Toshie Takahama, a broadcaster who spoke excellent English. Lillian Oppenhimer arranged for the Japanese to meet American folders and Mrs Takahama was struck by the free and equal way in which American, both experienced and novices associated, with none of the formal relationship of master and pupil that was traditional in Japan.

When she returned to Japan, Toshie Takahama determined to introduce this new approach to Japan and two years later she formed a new group called Sosaku Origami Group, 67. Among the members were Kunihiko Kasahara and Mitsunobu Sonobe. The Sosaku Origami Group was influential beyond its numbers and was an important factor in developing relationships between folders in Japan and the West and in introducing the new Western discoveries to Japan. The cross-fertilisation was to have the dramatic consequences for origami throughout the world.

Communication between Japan and the West flourished and new styles developed. One of the first Japanese folders of the new wave was Dokuohtei Nakano, who published his ideas in 1970 in the form of correspondence courses in Japanese and English. He combined parts of different bases in the subdivisions of the basic square and created a vast, but flexible system of bases for his models, most of which were birds and animals.

Another Japanese folder was Shuzo Fujimoto. With a mathematical background, Fujimoto developed many dazzling new ideas in origami, including twist folding, origami tessellations, polyhedra and representations of molecular structures. He also greatly advanced zigzag folding.

In many ways the work of the Japanese Jun Maekawa resembled that of the Americans, Robert Lang and John Montroll (see below). Like them, he followed the basic concept of the classic bases, but developed them in new extended ways. Kunihiko Kasahara had begun as a creative folder in the general manner of Yoshizawa, but at some point he came to recognize the importance that mathematics could play in folding. He immediately recognized Maekawa's genius and in 1983 he selflessly sponsored the publication of *Viva Origami*, a large book in Japanese entirely devoted to Maekawa's folds. The book was popular in the West and was followed by *Top Origami*, which explored the application of mathematics to origami. It featured not only Maekawa, but also other advanced folders from Japan and the West. Translated into English as *Origami for the Connoisseur*, it was very influential in spreading the new concepts of origami.

In America in 1988 Peter Engel wrote *Folding the Universe*. It included a study of the mathematics underlying the classic bases and showed how to create complex new bases. which made possible the folding of insects and sea creatures.

Robert Lang and John Montroll jointly wrote *Origami Sea Life* in 1989. They, too, used advanced bases. Both books took the art of folding to hitherto unimagined areas of complexity. Crabs, murex shells, and even sea urchins could now be folded with all their legs, antennae, and spines. Lang and Montroll later separately wrote further books, which expanded their ideas about complex bases. Lang also took box-pleating to its limits and his Black Forest Cuckoo Clock remains one of the ultimate achievements of folding.

"Modular Origami" or "Unit Origami" (the piecing together of many similar modules) is another style, closely connected with mathematics, that has proved widely popular. Although there had been a few traditional examples of modular folding from the eighteenth century, it was the invention by Mitsunbu Sonobe of the Sonobe Module that made modular folding popular. The first steps forwards were taken by Steve Krimball in the United States in the 1970s and the idea suddenly took off throughout the world.

In 1983 a young Japanese folder, Tomoko Fuse came to the notice of Western folders. Her style of unit origami was quite different. She concentrated on boxes that used a few large modules rather than on the assembly of many small units. The elegance of her models quickly attracted to her style folders who would not otherwise have been interested in modular folding.

In the late 1980s, Jun Maekawa and Robert Lang both published scientific articles on the new mathematical concepts of origami and in the early 1990s Lang created "Treemaker," a program for Macintosh computers, designed to assist in the creation of bases specific to the creature to be folded. The combination of mathematics with the newly advanced techniques for creating bases has also been taken up in Japan by young folders who are often mathematicians or scientists. They formed a very influential new society named "Origami Tanteidan," which means "The Origami Detectives."

Lest it be thought that complexity of one sort or another has overtaken origami, it should be pointed out that many folders continue to admire simplicity. Minimal Folding (the folding of a model with the minimum number of folds) and Pure Land Folding are also popular. Pure Land Folding is a style devised by John S. Smith of Britain. By using only mountain and valley folds and by avoiding reverse folds, it is aimed at simplifying origami for children and handicapped folders.

The development of technique has not been confined to devising new and ever more complex crease patterns. The process of folding itself has been developed. Wet folding follows the example of Akira Yoshizawa, who advocated the damping of the paper before or during folding. This technique enables the paper to be molded or sculpted, and life to be breathed into a model. It has been adopted by many modern folders, including David Brill of Britain, with his animals; the Italian, Alfredo Giunta, with his insects, and the American, Michael La Fosse.

The concept of origami sculpture has also been developed, mainly in France, where it has raised origami to the level of a fine art. Jean-Claude Correia has created many impressive textured wall hangings, which use a method of double pleating. Eric Joisel has achieved general acclaim for his Armadillo and his sculptural heads, which use quite simple origami techniques to achieve stunning results. Vincent Floderer has created a diversity of paper sculptures resembling mushrooms, leafless tree forms, and corals. Some of them appear to be remote from origami, yet they are still firmly rooted in basic paper-folding techniques. Another paper

sculptor is the Briton Paul Jackson, who uses a cross-pleating technique to create elegant, textured bowls. Jackson has also studied the aesthetic curves induced in a square of paper by one or two creases that only partially cross it.

The developments during the last 50 years in what was once mainly a children's pastime are remarkable. This can be explained by the vastly improved communications across the world as a whole, and especially the invention of the Internet and the World Wide Web. Origami societies have facilitated friendships across the globe through their magazines and their annual, and sometimes biennial, conventions at which folders have been able to meet in person to discuss new ideas.

A glimpse into the future of origami

By the beginning of the 1970s, people were starting to think that all that could be known about origami had already been discovered. How wrong they were! Origami has continued to develop many once-unimagined new techniques and to diversify into a galaxy of different styles. Where will the next developments be?

Could this be in the use of circular paper and curved creases? The use of circular paper has always appeared to be irrelevant because when a circle is folded over, it always makes a straight line, and straight lines form the same patterns no matter what the shape of the paper. Yet curved creases are now made in paper, through techniques such as tension creasing and not by the simple process of folding. So this may be the next development. There are already some folders who are beginning to explore the possibilities of curved creases and circular origami. But if the experience of the past 50 years is anything to go by, we are likely to be greatly surprised by the new origami of the future.

Essentials

Following diagrams

Origami diagrams use a standard set of symbols and phrases, originally developed by Akira Yoshizawa and extended by Robert Harbin and Sam Randlett. These symbols, which are entirely independent of language, may well be the single most significant factor in the spread of origami around the world. Once you have learned the basic set, you can then start to fold from diagrams drawn that are anywhere, making origami a truly worldwide activity.

Any crease made in a sheet of paper creates two folds at the same time – a valley fold, where the paper folds toward you and a mountain fold, where the paper folds away from you. An arrow is added to show in which direction the paper should move. These three elements alone are sufficient to make, and follow, many origami designs. If you add symbols for "turn the paper over," "pull some paper out," and "apply pressure," you can follow almost any diagram ever drawn!

A number of extra symbols have been developed to make the diagrams clearer, including "diagram scale increases," "diagram scale decreases," "rotate the paper," and "X-ray view." I have developed an extra symbol, "fold with feeling," to indicate that the folder should take special care at that stage. The phrase was frequently used in his many origami classes by the late Michael Shall, a wonderful origami motivator and enthusiast, .

The symbols illustrated in the column opposite are used throughout this book.

RIGHT: *These are the symbols you are most likely to need when following diagrams.*

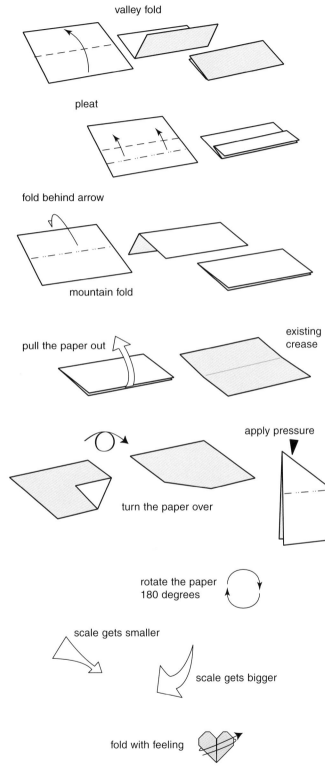

valley fold

pleat

fold behind arrow

mountain fold

pull the paper out

existing crease

apply pressure

turn the paper over

rotate the paper 180 degrees

scale gets smaller

scale gets bigger

fold with feeling

Paper

When practicing an origami model, you can use many different types of paper. The only limitations are that the paper should "hold" a crease and not be too thick for any multi-layered sequences. Fold the model over and over until you are confident with the sequence. When you have mastered the design and wish to make an exhibition-quality model, you need to think more carefully about the paper. Factors to consider include:

● The required size of the finished model – see how the practice sheet of paper compares with the size of the finished model and scale your "best" paper up accordingly. Remember, the larger the sheet of paper, the more the final model may sag under its own weight.

● The subject – animals may look better made in coarser paper in natural colors. A decorative vase may be better made from brighter paper; a car may look good from foil paper, while some designs are most elegant made from plain white paper. Use your judgment.

● The folding technique – complex models require paper that is both thin and strong. You will find out by experiment which types are suitable; get it wrong and the

paper will split or tear! If you wish to try wet folding a model, slightly thicker paper is often better. I really enjoy wet folding using "canson" paper, a French brand. Not only does it wet fold very well, but it comes in a useful range of colors and has a slight texture on one side.

Origami paper is ideal for practice since it is usually crisp and brightly colored. It is also suitable for decorative and modular designs. You will find that some models rely on the fact that origami paper is usually white on one side and colored on the other.

BELOW: *When practicing an origami model, you can use many different types of paper. The only limitations are that the paper should be able to hold a crease.*

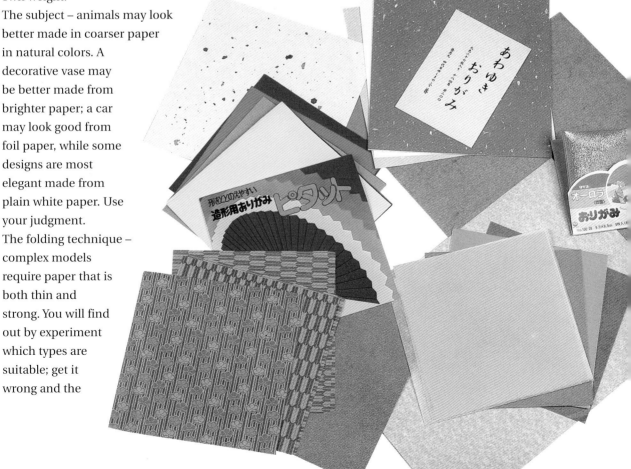

This contrast can be used on the finished model, but many origami artists won't use origami paper for serious folding. Each will have their own preferred type of paper, depending on the model they are making. The American artist, Michael La Fosse, actually makes his own individual sheets of paper, combining different ingredients to achieve the result he has in mind.

Whichever type of paper you choose, the most important thing is to make sure it is perfectly square. If you buy large sheets, you'll need a paper cutter to trim them down to size. If you are confident, a craft knife, steel ruler, and cutting board can be used, but please be careful!

Folding tips

There are a number of things you can do to achieve success when following origami diagrams:

- Fold with someone else – you can help each other!
- Check a couple of steps in advance, to get an idea of where you're going.
- Relax and take your time.
- Rotate your paper after each step if necessary, so it matches the next diagram.
- If you get really stuck, start with a fresh sheet – your folding will be neater and this may help you progress.
- Check that you are doing what the diagram says and not what your fingers want to do!
- Use a large sheet of paper – there's no point making life more difficult than it is.
- Fold on a flat surface where you will not feel cramped.
- Make sure the lighting is adequate.

LEFT: *Don't throw away half-finished creations, come back to them after a few months and look at them again.*

Bases

IN ORIGAMI THERE are standard sequences of folds that arrange the paper so that it offers a number of points and layers. Each sequence produces what we call a "base." Because many origami designs start from a base, it allows us to keep instructions shorter; can often omit several opening steps, and say, for example, "start with a Bird base." Many origami books also include a section devoted to the common bases. For aspiring creators, it can be easier to develop your own models by starting with a base, rather than from a plain square.

For people who are new to origami, bases are ideal for practicing the techniques required to fold properly. As you fold the base, unfold and refold each step, looking closely at how the paper moves, which corners or sides meet up, how it affects the shape of the paper, how many layers are formed, and so forth. Try turning a base inside out! Bases are wonderful examples of logical, natural folding sequences and can be enjoyed in their own right.

Kite Base

With only three creases, the Kite base is the simplest of the traditional bases.

1   Start with a square and fold it in half from corner to opposite corner. Crease and unfold.
2   Fold two adjacent sides to meet the diagonal crease.
3   The completed base.

You can see clearly where the base gets its name from! Although this is a very simple origami sequence, folders have discovered many wonderful creations using it as their starting point.

Blintz Base

This is another simple base, which allegedly takes its name from a Jewish pastry-making technique. Since the essence of the base is to fold four corners to the center, you first need to establish where the center is. You can do this by folding in half from side to side, or corner to corner, both ways. However, folding to the center in this way often leads to slight errors—the last corner doesn't always meet the first one neatly. To get round this, we fold to an edge rather than to a crease.

1   Start with a square and fold it in half from side to side. Unfold.
2   Fold in half using the other two sides. This establishes the center of the square.
3   Fold two outside (short) edges to lie along the top (folded) edge. Repeat on the other side.
4   Unfold the layers from underneath.
5   The completed Blintz base.

OPPOSITE: *Although simple, the Kite and Blintz bases are fundamental starting points for many designs.*

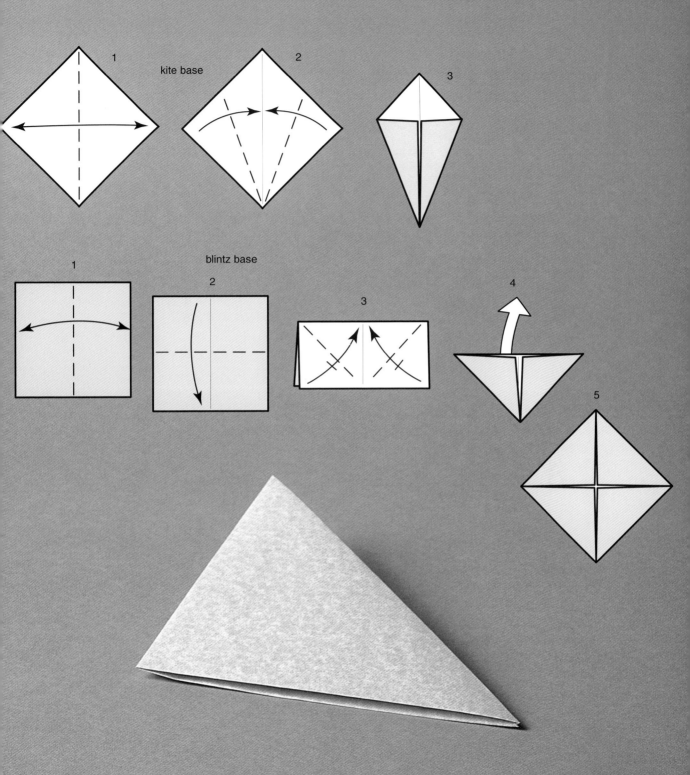

kite base

1

2

3

blintz base

1

2

3

4

5

Fish Base

This takes the Kite base a step further. As with many bases, there is more than one way in which to fold it. I find the following sequence most satisfying.

1   Start with a square and crease
    both diagonals.
2   Fold two sides to the central crease.
3   This is the Kite base. Turn the paper over.
4   Fold the pointed end to the opposite
    corner.
5   This is the result. Turn the paper over.

6   Place your finger inside a pocket, opening one
    of the corners. As you do so, fold the raw
    (original) edge to meet the diagonal crease.
7   Like this. Repeat the move on the other side.
8   The completed base.

This method does produce creases that are not strictly necessary. As shown in the boxed area, you can fold the long valleys only up to the diagonal. When a corner is formed into a point in this way, it is called a "Rabbit's Ear."

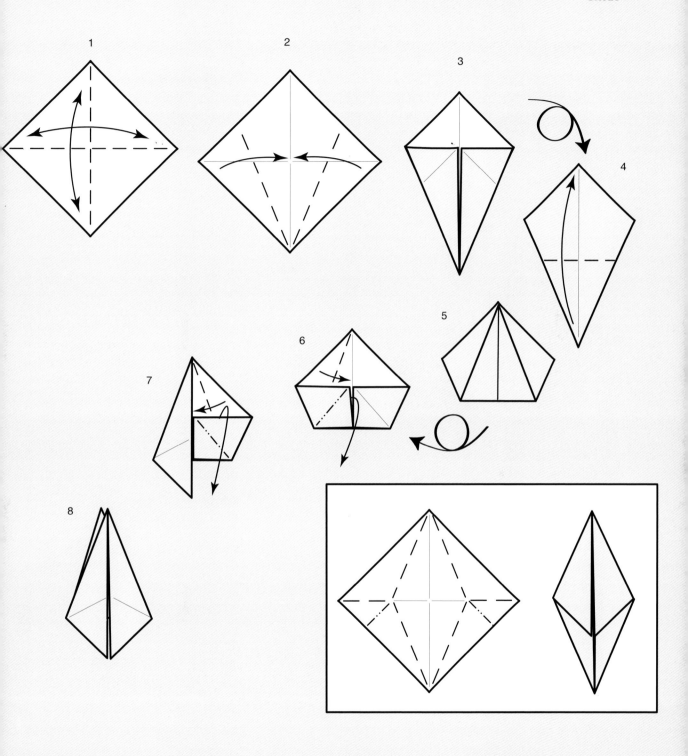

Preliminary Base

This combination of four creases opens up many folding possibilities, since it creates five points in addition to the original four corners! The only important thing to remember is that the diagonals and side-to-side creases need to be on opposite sides of the paper.

1 Start with a square, colored side upward. Crease both diagonals.
2 Turn the paper over and crease side to side both ways.
3 Rotate the paper and use the creases shown to bring the top corner toward you as the side points fold inward.
4 The completed base.

Another, somewhat unexpected route can be used to fold a Preliminary base:

5 Start with a square, white side face upward, creased in half sideways. Fold in half from bottom to top.
6 Fold the bottom right corner to the upper middle and fold the lower left behind to the same point.
7 Put your fingers in the central pocket and open out, gently pressing the sides together. You will end up with an (upside-down) Preliminary base.

Waterbomb Base

This base takes its name from the traditional waterbombs you may have played with at school.

1 Start with a square, colored side upward. Crease side to side both ways.
2 Turn the paper over and crease both diagonals.
3 Use the creases shown to bring the top corners and sides toward you as the upper edge folds down.
4 The completed base.

You may have noticed that we have used exactly the same creases as for the Preliminary base, but we have folded the creases from the other side of the paper. Either of these two bases can be turned inside out to form the other. Try it – it's fun!

Can you work out how to fold a Waterbomb base using a method similar to the second method given for the Preliminary base?

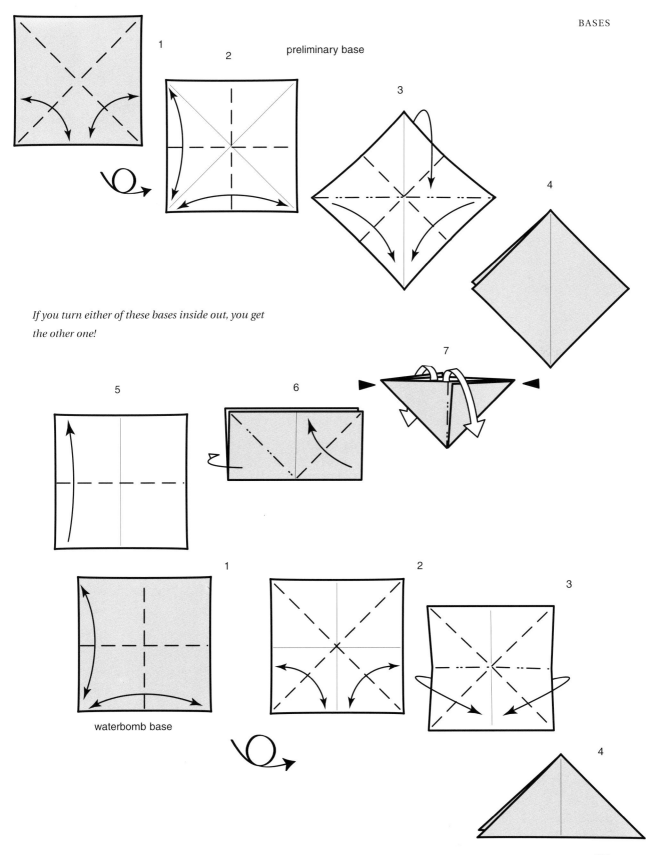

preliminary base

1

2

3

4

If you turn either of these bases inside out, you get the other one!

5

6

7

1

waterbomb base

2

3

4

31

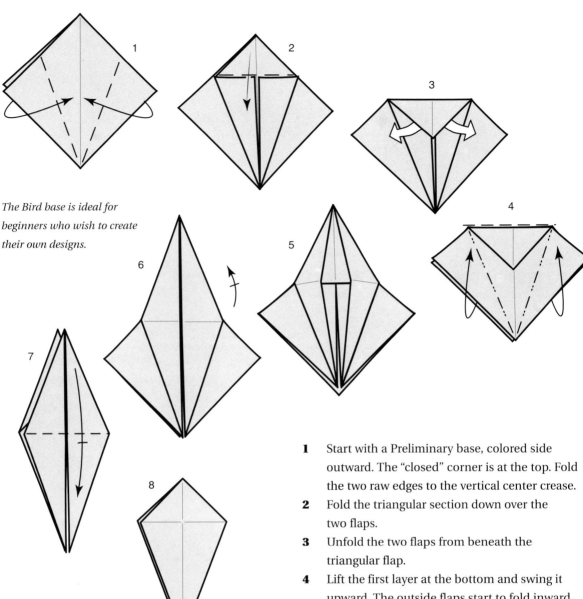

The Bird base is ideal for beginners who wish to create their own designs.

Bird Base

The Bird base makes use of a wonderful technique called a "petal fold." The base is perhaps best known as the one from which the Flapping Bird and the traditional Crane are made, but it has been used for a wide variety of origami subjects.

1 Start with a Preliminary base, colored side outward. The "closed" corner is at the top. Fold the two raw edges to the vertical center crease.

2 Fold the triangular section down over the two flaps.

3 Unfold the two flaps from beneath the triangular flap.

4 Lift the first layer at the bottom and swing it upward. The outside flaps start to fold inward.

5 This is the petal fold in progress. You will need to ease it gently flat while reinforcing the outside edges of the top section.

6 This is the completed fold. Repeat steps 4–6 on the other side.

7 Fold the upper flap downward, repeating behind.

8 The completed base.

If you unfold a Bird base, you will see many possibilities for using the creases in different ways to create new designs.

Multiform Base

This sequence of folds produces a square with four flaps that can be swung to either side. This can produce many different shapes, as well as providing as the starting point for more complex designs.

1   Start with an unfolded Waterbomb base, turn it over and fold a Blintz base then return to the original side.

2   Fold each side in to the center, crease, and unfold.

3   Using the creases shown, start to fold the halfway points of each side in toward the center. You don't need any extra creases.

4   This is one state of the Multiform base. More commonly, you open each corner using the crease shown.

5   Open the other corners in the same way.

6   This is another state of the Multiform base.

By swinging the flaps either way as well as folding the central square in half from side to side or along a diagonal, you can produce a number of different shapes. See how many you can make.

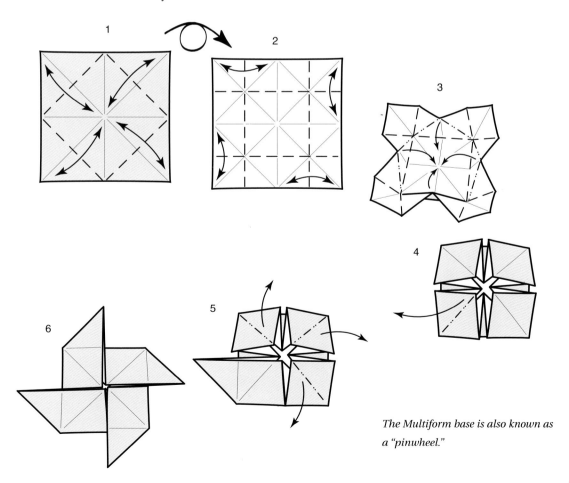

The Multiform base is also known as a "pinwheel."

New geometry – creating an angle of 60 degrees

Traditional bases generally use 90, 45, and 22.5 degree angles. However, creative folders have begun to explore 60 (and hence 30 and 15) degree geometry. This yields new shapes and many as yet unexplored possibilities. An angle of 60 degrees is surprisingly easy to create using origami.

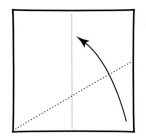

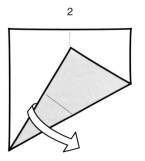

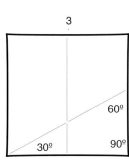

1 Start with a square that has been folded in half from side to side. Fold the lower right corner to touch the crease, making the crease start from the lower left corner.

2 Unfold again.

3 The crease has created angles of 30 and 60 degrees.

We can use the same geometry to divide a side into thirds.

4 When you make the second crease, don't crease it all the way, but pinch a small crease where the crease passes through the folded edge.

5 Fold the lower right corner to the pinch mark, creasing only the lower end of the fold.

6 Unfold the last crease.

7 The last crease you made marks the point one-third along the lower edge. Using it, we can easily add vertical creases to divide the square into three equal sections.

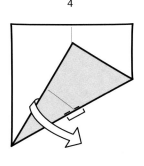

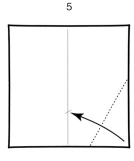

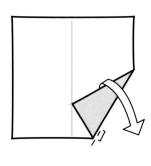

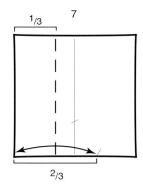

Using thirds and 60-degree angles will open up new areas for exploration.

Hexagon

Although much origami is folded from squares, there are designs that utilize other formats. The A4 rectangle has been employed for folding purposes. As well as offering a "square with extra paper at one end," this format has revealed a fascinating underlying geometry that has produced some versatile origami modules, such as the A4 Rhombic Unit (see page 99). Other shapes that have been explored include triangles, pentagons and hexagons. The English folder, David Brill, has produced a very elegant horse and a family of lions using a triangle. Few folders have explored pentagons or hexagons, other than for folding flowers and dishes.

1. Start with a square with a diagonal crease. Fold one end of the diagonal to the other.
2. Add short creases to mark the half and quarter way points on the double raw edge.
3. Starting the crease at the center of the folded edge, fold the halfway mark so it lies on the quarter-way crease.
4. Fold the lower flap over the top of the upper.
5. Cut the top section between where the layers overlap. This will be at right angles to the vertical. Open out for a hexagon.

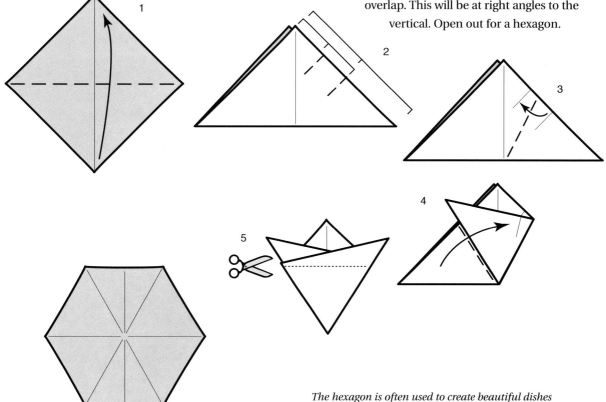

The hexagon is often used to create beautiful dishes and bowls.

Crease patterns

One fascinating aspect of bases is that they can reveal the underlying geometry of traditional origami. All we need to do is unfold the base back to the square, revealing what is known as the "crease pattern" in it. With many of the bases, it can be seen that the crease pattern can be broken down into a simple pattern that is duplicated as the bases grow more complex.

Starting with the Kite base, if we rotate the upper shaded triangle about point O, we create the shaded section of the Fish base. We can see the same shape as a smaller section of the Fish base and if we make the Frog base, it appears yet again. We also find that miniature Kite and Bird bases appear within more complex structures. In a similar way, the basic elements of the Preliminary (and Waterbomb) bases appear as part of the Blintz and Multiform bases.

This repetitive symmetry allows us to use similar techniques throughout the folding of a model, even when it becomes complicated. The same crease patterns are present and so the same techniques, with suitable manipulation of the layers and edges, can be used. The patterns also reveal the fundamental "division by two" geometry typical of many traditional designs. We start with 90 degrees, then divide it into two, creating an angle of 45 degrees. This is further bisected into 22.5 degrees.

Bases as a barrier

While bases are essential for a large number of origami models, they can also be seen as a potential barrier to new designs. By utilizing existing bases and techniques, it is less likely that you will develop new ideas and models. Many designers deliberately avoid standard bases, preferring to develop a unique base for each design, arranging the paper in the optimum way to produce the required points and flaps. American master folder Robert Lang has taken this approach a step farther, creating a software program called Treemaker (see page 20) which, when given certain parameters (such as number and position of points), will generate a crease pattern that could be used to create such a base.

However, as with music, a mastery of technique allows you to express your ideas with fewer restraints. Knowledge of traditional origami geometry, while not essential, is a useful tool to have at your disposal. The important point is to not allow traditional technique to dominate your thinking. Creative paper-folders should be open to a wide variety of influences.

A good example of this is the work of Vincent Floderer (see the Gallery), a French folder who has taken the origami world by storm with his "crumpled" organic paper sculptures and forms. Although on first appearance his work might seem to be completely free of traditional techniques, on closer investigation many of his designs do indeed reflect familiar crease patterns after all.

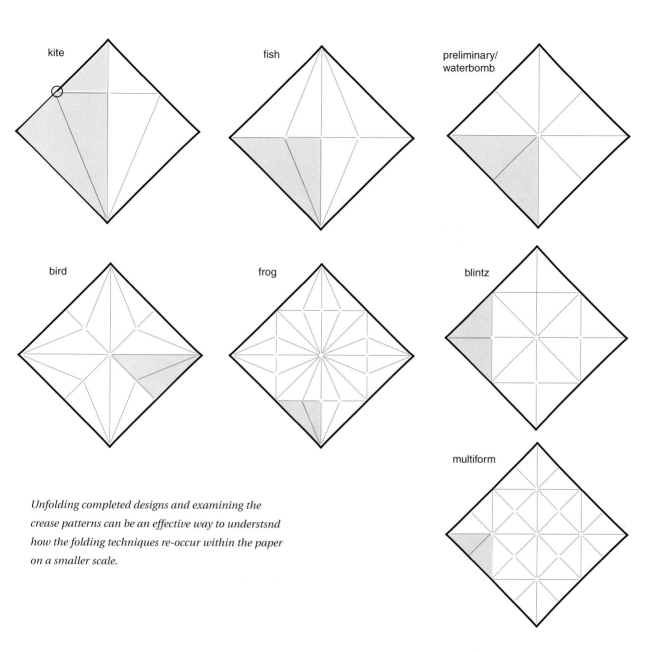

kite

fish

preliminary/
waterbomb

bird

frog

blintz

multiform

Unfolding completed designs and examining the
crease patterns can be an effective way to understsnd
how the folding techniques re-occur within the paper
on a smaller scale.

Creativity

SOME PAPER-FOLDERS are happy making other people's designs and developing a wide range of origami skills and techniques. Others specialize in making large models or tiny ones. Some enjoy the challenge of folding 300 identical units for an elaborate modular construction. However, to my mind, perhaps the most enjoyable and satisfying aspect of origami is creating your own designs.

You don't need to be blessed with a deep vein of artistic talent (although it probably helps!), but simply with a desire to discover something hidden within the paper. There are a number of approaches people use to create origami. No one approach is necessarily better than another and all are equally valid. It's a matter of finding the one that works for you.

Doodling

This is a little like seeing faces in the clouds – you play with the paper, folding flaps this way and that, until a subject begins to emerge. You can then begin to exercise a little more control and direction to your folding, until you have something that (hopefully) looks like the intended subject. Very often, this approach works best when you start with an existing base, or perhaps with a model by someone else that is half-finished. Never throw anything away – keep an "ideas" box to store all your doodles. Very often you can revisit them later and see a new idea in them.

Adapting

If you make enough changes to someone else's design, you may well come up with an original model! It's good manners to credit the source of your inspiration when you teach or diagram the model. Don't be surprised if an experienced folder can spot your sources immediately!

Conceptual

Some folders are able to take a given subject, analyze where it will need flaps, points, and so on, then mentally work back to the original square. This requires an extensive knowledge of origami techniques and a certain way of thinking!

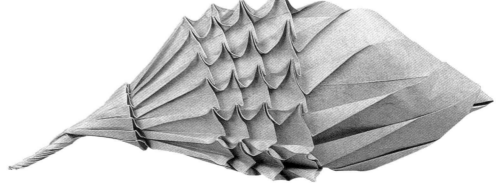

Engineering

Some types of subject lend themselves to folding using a "mechanical" method, breaking them down into shapes and configurations that you already know you can achieve by using certain techniques. These designs are usually very logical and satisfying to fold. An extension of this approach is the use of computer software programs to generate potential crease patterns.

What makes a good design?

Like any other artform, origami devotees argue passionately about what they believe to be the "best" form of origami. Some prefer complex designs that incorporate all the physical features of the subject, often taking several hundred steps to diagram. For them, accuracy is key and everything else is secondary. Others, like myself, aim to capture the essence of the subject as simply as possible and present an almost "cartoon-like" representation of the subject. Others enjoy making multi-piece, modular designs. Some accept cutting as part of origami; others use glue to hold models together. I believe that all these forms are valid and have their place in the spectrum of paper art.

As you work your way through models and books, you will inevitably find your tastes and preferences change, just as your tastes change in many areas of life. The most important thing is to appreciate and accept the views of others, even if you don't like the origami they produce. You should never close your eyes and ears to techniques, influences, or ideas – give them a chance and they may well help your own origami to develop a style of its own.

Finally

Once you have a finished model that you feel is original and has potential, you should fold it again and again, looking for an elegant folding sequence and location points for the creases, and generally refining it. At this stage, try to produce diagrams to remind you how to fold it. These don't have to be wonderful – just enough to jog your memory if you don't fold it again for some weeks. Once you're happy with the model and sequence, you can take the time to produce proper diagrams to distribute to other folders. Computers are often used for this purpose and modern software can help you produce professional results.

Lastly, don't be depressed if you discover that "your" model has already been discovered by another folder. This is inevitable, since there are many thousands of folders, all using the same bases and techniques. The important thing is that you found it through your own efforts. As your experience grows, you'll start to avoid areas that may be overworked (such as elephants, penguins, and modular rings) and will study more obscure subjects and techniques.

Technique

THE BASIS OF any technical ability is a sound knowledge of the fundamental skills that are needed. Origami is no different: if you want to fold complex designs, you need to start with simple ones. You must begin to feel confident in your ability to make precise creases, to interpret diagrams, and to fold neatly. If you have creative ambitions, a wide knowledge of existing designs and techniques will allow you to steer a path away from traditional work and to develop your own identity.

This chapter contains designs that are fairly simple, but they will give you a good grounding in folding techniques. All the creases will have location points and can be folded flat, except for the final design, for which you will venture into the world of three-dimensional folding.

Octagonal Crown

Design by Nick Robinson

This design is an ideal project with which to practice accurate, neat creasing. With a little ingenuity, this apparently unpromising fold can be used in a variety of creative ways.

1 Start with a square and fold one corner to the opposite corner.

2 Fold one end of the long folded edge to the other, crease and unfold.

3 Fold each end of the same edge to the center, crease and unfold. This completes the unit. Make three more the same.

4 Slide one unit inside another so that the first set of vertical creases overlap.

5 Make sure the creases overlap exactly, and fold the sides at 90 degrees to each other.

6 Join another two units in the same way, and join the double units to each other.

7 Form the long vertical creases (the original diagonals) into mountain creases to complete the octagonal crown.

8 The completed crown.

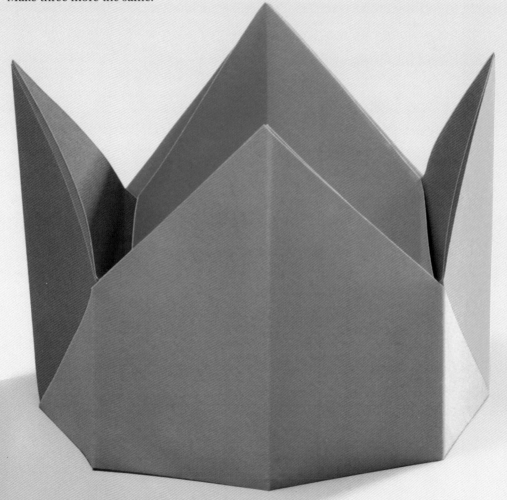

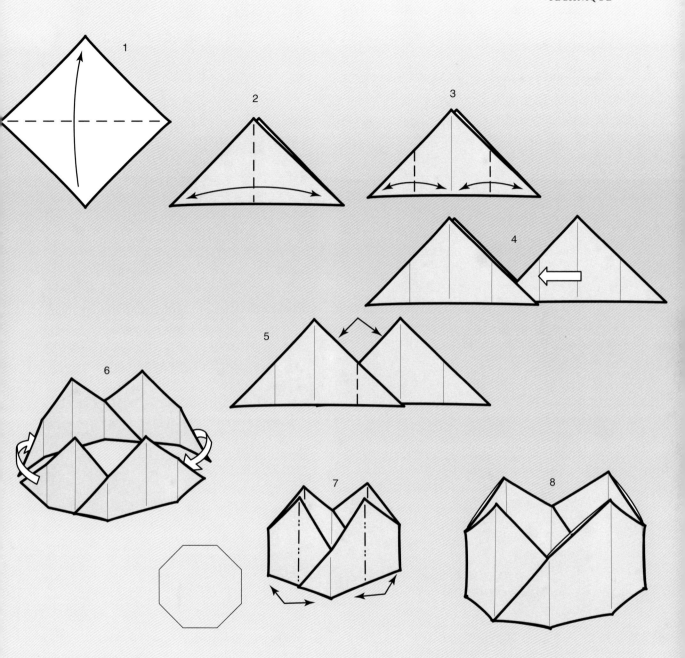

Creative challenge

If you can avoid making the long crease in step 2, you can create a four-sided crown that holds together very firmly. To do this, you need to make a tiny pinch-mark to locate the center for step 3. A less direct way might be to fold a "spare" unit to use as a template for locating the center.

90-45-degree Set Square

Design by Nick Robinson

The Crown on page 42 is "open"–in other words, its flaps are not held closed by any folding techniques. This design has the same profile, but the shape is "closed" by folding techniques. It will work from almost any rectangle of paper. The result is a set square with 90- and 45-degree corners, with which you can explore basic geometry and tessellation (the combination of shapes to form a tiled effect).

1   Start with a sheet of A4 ($8^1/4$ x $11^2/3$ inches) and fold a short edge to lie along the longer edge.
2   Fold two corners to lie along the inside raw edge.
3   Fold along the raw edge, crease firmly, and unfold.
4   Fold the large triangle in half.
5   Open the pocket slightly and carefully tuck the smaller section inside.

Creative challenge

Unfold the paper back to the very start and see if you can create the same result, using the same creases but in a different order, perhaps changing valley to mountain and vice versa. This design can also be used to make a very practical bookmark – make sure you use decorative paper. Experiment to find the ideal size of starting paper.

The "bonus" crease pattern shows you all the creases you need to create your own 30-60-90-degree set square. Use the technique shown on page 34 to create the initial angle, which starts at the bottom left corner, then discover the sequence that creates a locked set square. As a clue, the shaded section stays on the table at the end.

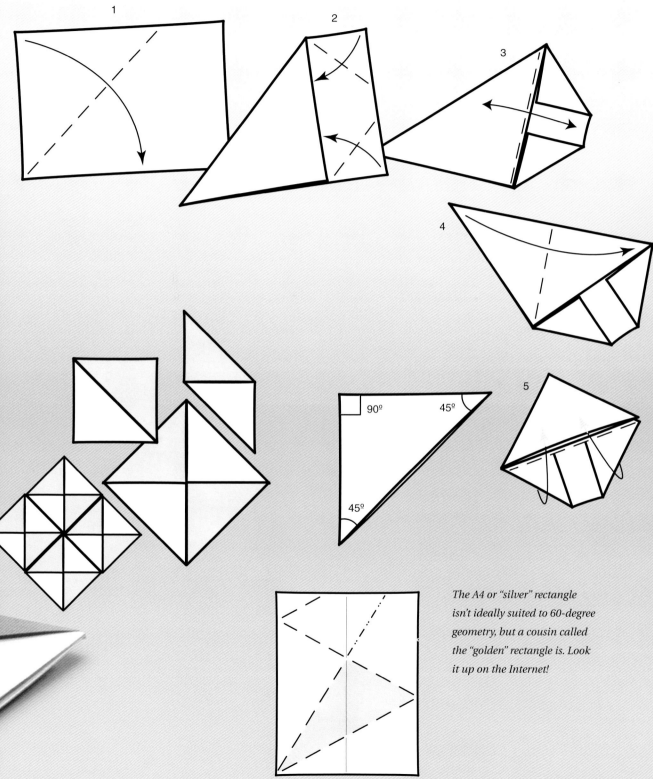

1

2

3

4

90°   45°

45°

5

The A4 or "silver" rectangle isn't ideally suited to 60-degree geometry, but a cousin called the "golden" rectangle is. Look it up on the Internet!

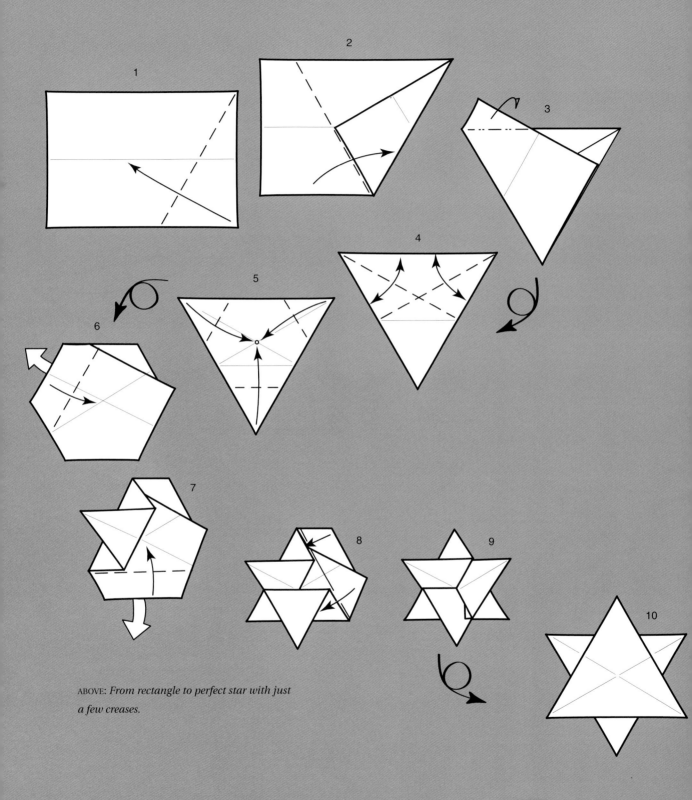

ABOVE: *From rectangle to perfect star with just a few creases.*

A4 Star

Design by various

This design makes use of 60-degree geometry instead of the more conventional 22.5-degree geometry. This gives an equilateral triangle, from which it is a short step to a six-pointed star.

1 Start with a sheet of A4, or similar rectangle, creased in half. Fold the lower right corner to touch the center crease, making sure the new crease starts at the top right corner. See page 34 for more about geometry.

2 Fold the lower left corner over to lie along the folded edge.

3 This gives us most of the triangle. Fold the small flap over the edge underneath and tuck it between the layers.

4 Turn the paper over. Fold two adjacent edges together to bisect the angle of the corner. Repeat with one other corner. These two creases establish the center of the triangle.

5 Fold each of the corners in to the center. Turn the paper over.

6 The paper is now very nearly a perfect hexagon. Fold the top left edge in to the center of the triangle, allowing the point to "flip out" from underneath.

7 Repeat step 6 with the lower edge.

8 Finally, fold in the third section, tucking the upper end underneath the layer of the first section to hold it in place.

9 The completed star.

10 Turn it over to reveal the "clean" side.

Creative challenge

Can you make this design easily from a square? If not, work out the optimum shape of the rectangle that you need.

Multiform Fish

Design by various

The Multiform base lives up to its name when you start to play with its various possibilities. This simple fish is made by adding only six creases to the base.

1 Start with the Multiform base, opened into the pinwheel position (see page 33). Swing over the lower two points so they face the other way.

2 Fold the bottom right corner to the center.

3 Fold the small triangular flap down.

4 This is the half-finished tail. Repeat on the other half.

5 Leaving a small gap, fold both remaining flaps over. The width of the gap is not important.

6 This is the result.

7 Turn the paper over for the completed fish.

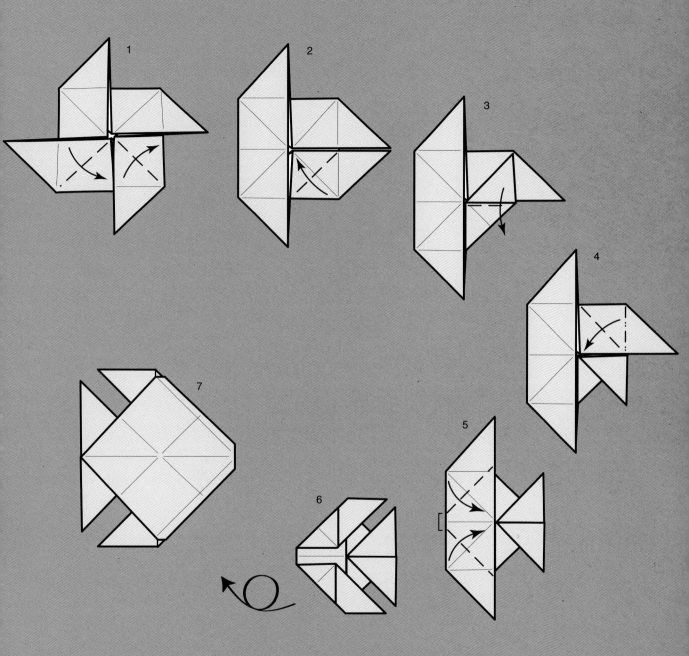

Creative challenge

Try to fold the fish in such a way that there are as few creases on the body as possible. To do this, you'll need to unfold the fish and work out which creases are essential, then find alternative ways of folding to avoid non-essential creases.

Horse's Head (a)

Design by David Brill

David Brill, an origami artist of extraordinary talent, developed this design. He starts with a basic design, then adds a subtle but interesting "lock" and finally, in the wet-folding section (see Horse's

Head (b) page 114), shows how to add subtle three-dimensional shaping to produce a sophisticated and elegant result.

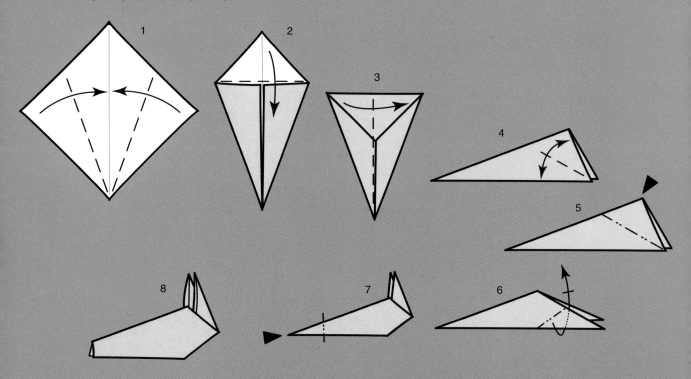

By altering the amount folded during step 7, you can make other types of animal.

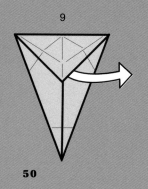

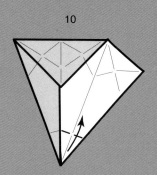

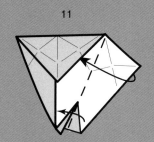

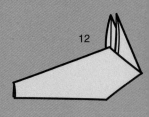

1 Start with a square, white face upward, creased in half. Fold two sides in to the center.

2 This is the Kite base. Fold the top triangle down.

3 Fold in half from left to right.

4 Rotate the paper to this position. Fold the shortest edge to meet the longest edge, crease and unfold.

5 Make an inside-reverse fold on the corner, using the creases made in the step 4.

6 Mountain-fold both sharp points inside the head to form the ears.

7 Make an inside-reverse fold on the nose section to blunt it.

8 Open the ears slightly for the completed head.

To lock the nose

This technique is very useful to prevent flaps from coming undone.

9 Open the finished model back to step 3, and open the right-hand flap.

10 Fold the nose section over on the right-hand side only.

11 Refold the right-hand flap, tucking it over the small flap at the nose end as you fold the paper in half again. Re-form the ears.

11 The finished head.

51

Tree

Design by Nick Robinson

This design makes use of 60-degree geometry to create a natural form. There are very few origami designs like this, so it is an area ripe for exploration if you want to create truly original designs. The shaping creases at the end can be varied to produce a variety of different profiles.

1   Start with a square, folded in half both ways. Fold the bottom left corner to touch the horizontal crease, starting this fold at the top left corner.

2   Like this. Unfold and repeat with the lower right corner.

3   Fold the crease farthest to the left back on itself, making the fold pass through the intersection of creases (see diagram 4 for guidance).

4   Unfold and repeat on the right-hand side.

5   Turn the paper over. Using only existing creases, fold the mountain creases into the vertical center, wrapping the lower tip of the paper underneath.

6   Fold the left-hand point to the right as far as it will easily go.

7   Fold the point back to the left, crease, and unfold.

8   Inside reverse-fold the point on the crease you have just made. This forms a shallow pocket.

9   Fold the right-hand point into the pocket that you have just made.

10 Turn the paper over. Shape the sides of the tree – these do not have to be symmetrical! Fold the tree trunk in half on either side, and open halfway to form a stand.

11 Turn over for the completed tree.

Creative challenge

Starting from step 6, can you create a squid or cuttlefish? The creases shown will give you a clue as to how to form four short tentacles at the front.

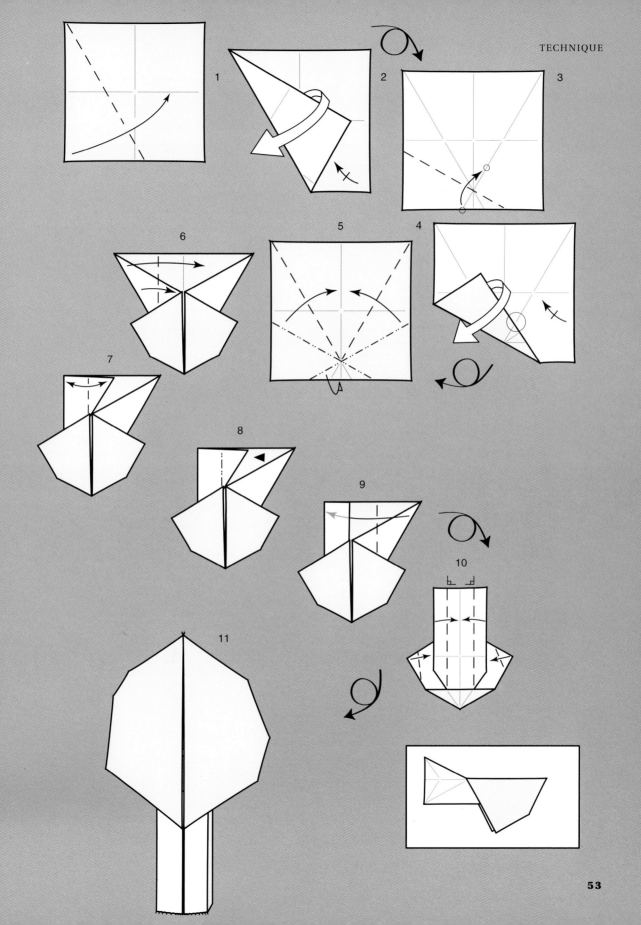

Silver Half-Cube

Design by Nick Robinson

When folding geometric shapes, it is important to make your creases very sharp and not extend them farther than they need to go.

1 Start with a sheet of A4, or similar rectangle, and divide the short side into thirds (see page 34 for guidance). Fold the short edge to the left-hand side, being careful to crease only outside the right-hand third crease. Repeat the move on the other side.

2 Fold the lower short edge to touch the creases made in step 1. Crease and unfold.

3 Fold the upper end of the short crease to touch the crease made in step 2. Crease and unfold.

4 Turn the paper over. Refold the horizontal crease only where shown, changing it to a valley from this side of the paper. Add the small diagonal creases.

5 Turn the paper over again. Match the lower creases in the next section. It is easier to fold the upper section down rather than the other way round!

6 Rotate the paper through 180 degrees and fold the left-hand side over.

7 Fold the mountain crease to the outside edge, forming a new valley crease. The paper becomes three-dimensional from here onward.

8 Repeat the last step on the right-hand side. This diagram shows the result. Carefully make a crease where the raw edge meets the folded edge.

9 Use the creases shown (no new ones please!) to collapse the paper toward you.

10 How the design looks as you progress.

11 When it has magically collapsed into a half-cube shape, carefully ease the flap into the awaiting pocket. Tighten all the creases.

12 The completed half-cube.

Creative challenge

Can you work out an easy way to create a suitably sized rectangle from a square? If that's too easy, can you find a way of adding (at an earlier stage) the crease needed in step 8, but using a different technique?

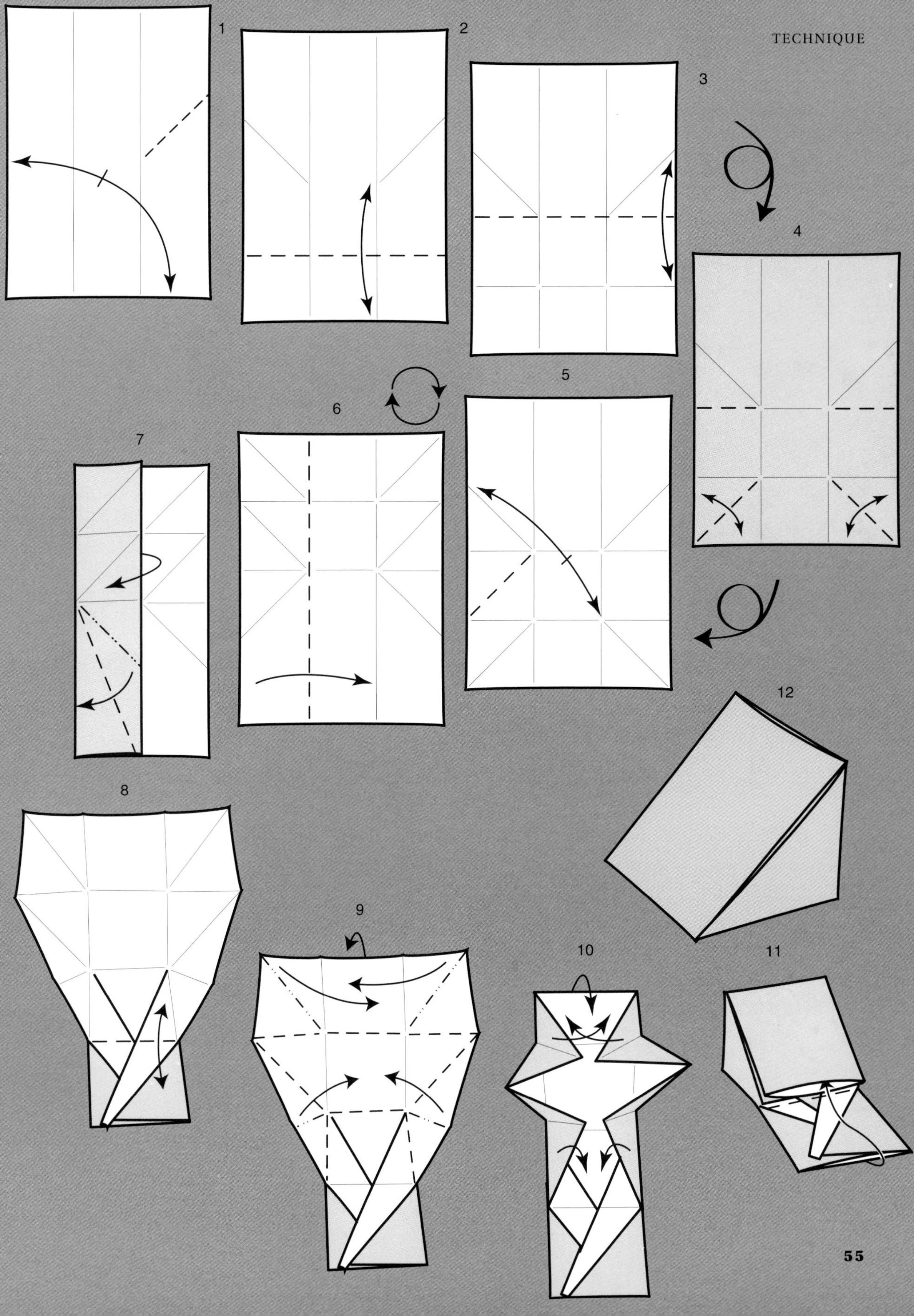

1

2

3

4

5

6

7

8

9

10

11

12

Practice

HAVING WORKED YOUR way through the Techniques section, you'll now be ready to extend your range of techniques and look at some more subtle designs. You'll tackle animals, paper planes, and even some origami humor! As you make the folds, unfold each step and refold it a few times. Try to work out what the creator of the design had in mind at any given stage and anticipate how that step will help toward achieving the final subject.

As you make any of the designs in this book, feel free to take off at a tangent whenever you have an idea. You can always come back and finish the model as diagrammed, but creative ideas should always be explored. After all, if you make enough changes to a given design, at some point it becomes an original. All creative paper folders owe a huge debt to the work of other creators and while we respect their work, hopefully we can also extend and build on it.

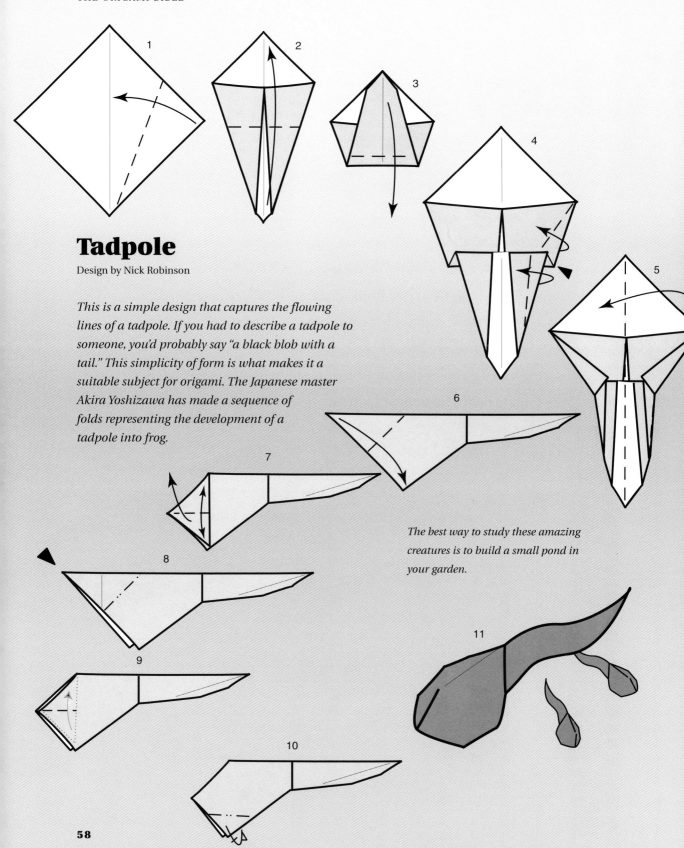

Tadpole

Design by Nick Robinson

This is a simple design that captures the flowing lines of a tadpole. If you had to describe a tadpole to someone, you'd probably say "a black blob with a tail." This simplicity of form is what makes it a suitable subject for origami. The Japanese master Akira Yoshizawa has made a sequence of folds representing the development of a tadpole into frog.

The best way to study these amazing creatures is to build a small pond in your garden.

1 Start with a square creased along a diagonal. Fold a corner in as if you were folding a Kite Base, but move the corner toward you a little along the central diagonal before creasing. Fold the opposite corner in to meet the first one.

2 Fold the "pointed" end to the opposite corner.

3 Leave a small gap, then fold the flap back down again.

4 This step is a little difficult. Start by folding the tail flap as shown. As the fold meets the pleat, put your finger inside the small pocket and ease it inside while making the other valley crease. Repeat on the other side.

5 This is the result. Next time, step 4 will be easier to perform! Fold the model in half along an existing crease.

6 Fold the front corner to touch the bottom corner.

7 Fold the small triangle in half, and open out the last two steps.

8 Push in the corner point so it lies between the outer layers. This move is known as an "inside reverse fold."

9 Refold the small crease made in step 7, but inside the model. This locks the paper together.

10 Round the body with two small mountain folds.

11 Open the body, curve the tail (by wrapping it around your finger and pressing firmly), and the model is complete.

Creative challenge

The first four steps can be adjusted to alter the proportions of the tadpole. See if you can produce a series of folds showing how the tadpole develops. Can you design a model with back legs?

Sheep

Design by Nick Robinson

Like a tadpole, a sheep has a rather vague outline – a round body, with a head at one end! This type of subject allows the creator wonderful freedom to achieve a fresh folding method. Here's the method I settled on, based on a simple dog design that I already had, filed away in my "in progress" box.

Step 5 is a move that I enjoy – the head and body almost form themselves. The moves that form the head (step 8 onward) require you to use your judgment about exactly where to make the folds. These folds are said to be made "by eye." They become easier with practice.

1 Start with a square, white side up, and crease both diagonals. Fold three corners to the center, fold the fourth corner in, crease and unfold it.

2 Fold the original corner in to a point about $3/4$ of the distance to the crease. Turn the paper over.

3 Fold the upper right edge to meet the vertical edge, but only crease the left-hand side of the paper. The dotted lines show where the crease could have extended.

4 Crease and unfold. Repeat on the other side.

5 You now have all the creases you need to form both the head and the body in one flowing move. Carefully follow the creases shown (see diagram 6 for guidance).

Unfold and refold this step until you are quite clear about what is happening. Enjoy the move!

6 Fold the corner of the tail over, crease, and unfold. Fold the upper flap over so that the inside edge meets the outside edge, crease, and unfold. Repeat on the flap behind.

7 Inside-reverse the tail corner. Fold the two lower corners in to match.

8 Now take a deep breath. Fold the lower layer at the front to the left. At the same time, fold the base of the head farther in so that it forms a slight angle to the edge underneath. Repeat behind.

9 This is (should be!) the result. Fold the lower part of the jaws underneath, front and back. Push in the top of the head (inside-reverse fold) as you did with the tail.

10 Do one more shaping fold on the head, front, and back.

11 The completed sheep.

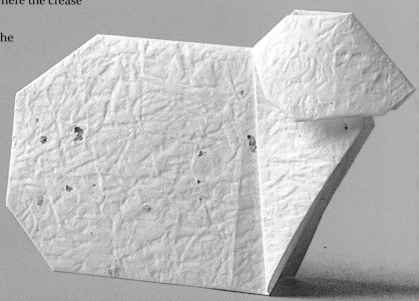

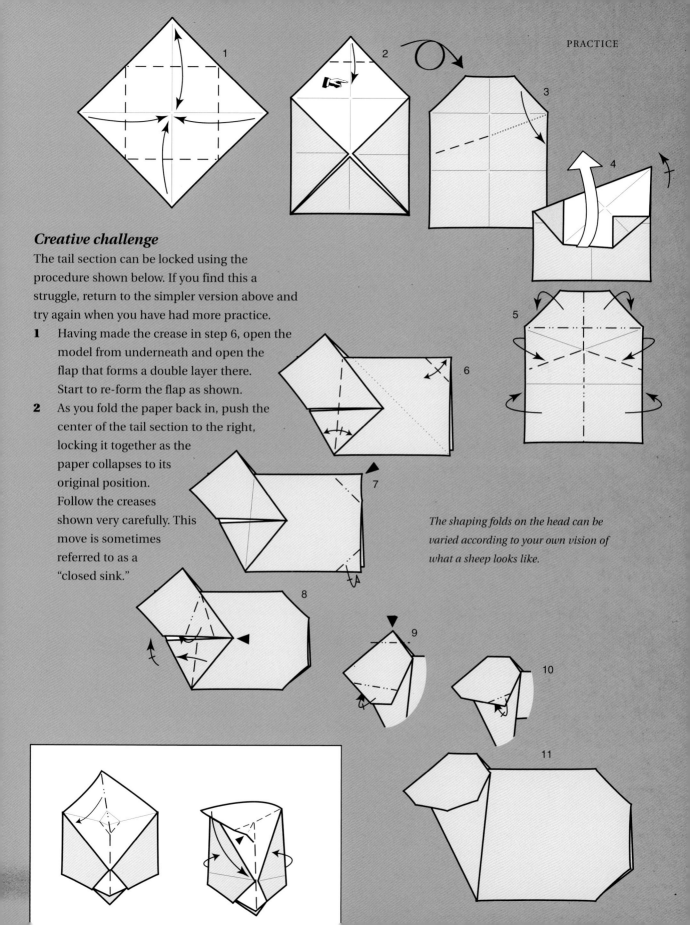

Creative challenge

The tail section can be locked using the
procedure shown below. If you find this a
struggle, return to the simpler version above and
try again when you have had more practice.

1   Having made the crease in step 6, open the
    model from underneath and open the
    flap that forms a double layer there.
    Start to re-form the flap as shown.

2   As you fold the paper back in, push the
    center of the tail section to the right,
    locking it together as the
    paper collapses to its
    original position.
    Follow the creases
    shown very carefully. This
    move is sometimes
    referred to as a
    "closed sink."

*The shaping folds on the head can be
varied according to your own vision of
what a sheep looks like.*

Tree Bear

Design by Nick Robinson

Origami isn't noted for its humor, but there most definitely is a fun side to paper folding! This design is part of a series I made, representing visual jokes (such as the "Mexican on a Bicycle") using paper. Initially, I made the whole thing from a single square, but the resulting complexity seemed out of character with the simple nature of the joke, so I developed it first from two sheets of paper and, finally, from three. It works better if you use slightly smaller paper than usual.

The bear's paws

1 Start with a square of crisp paper, colored side up. Fold in half from bottom to top.
2 Fold the top raw edge down on either side.
3 Fold either side in by one-fifth, so that the amount folded in is about the same as the gap left in the center. Use your own judgment – the exact distance isn't critical.
4 Fold bottom-right and top-left corners behind.
5 Round off two of the inside corners as well.
6 Finally, round off the remaining corners. The short edges on the inside should be about the same length.
7 Make two of these.

The tree

8 Start with a square the same size as used for the paws and fold in half from left to right.
9 Gently curve the paper and tuck it inside each of the bear's paws.
10 Slide the paws up and down the tree until they look lifelike.

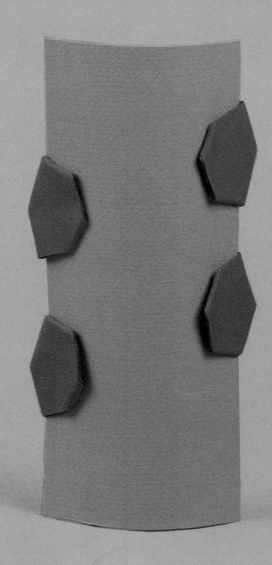

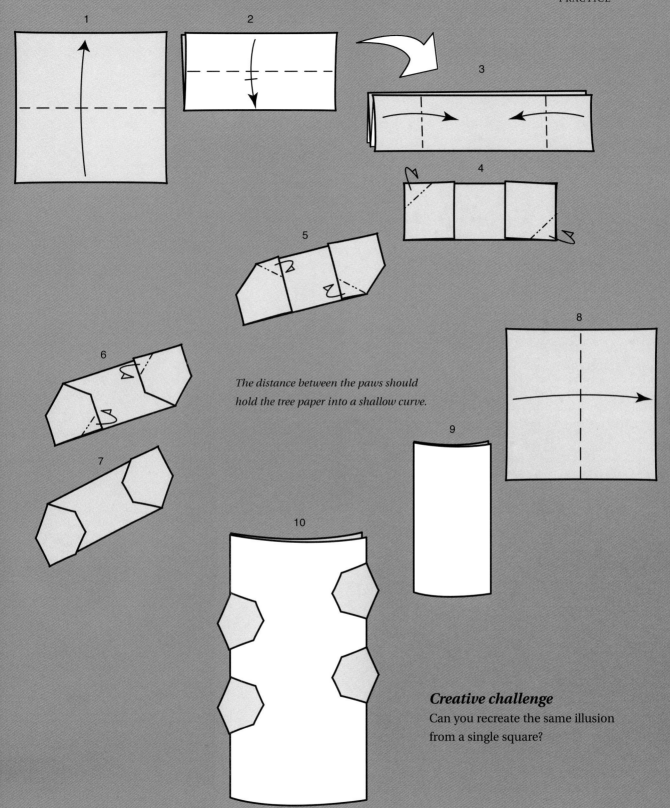

The distance between the paws should hold the tree paper into a shallow curve.

Creative challenge
Can you recreate the same illusion from a single square?

Mountains

Design by Nick Robinson

This design uses the two colors of the paper to depict the subject, as well as the actual shape. I call this approach "Painting with Paper." See "Gone Fishing" on page 92 for another example. After step 9, you can choose between two different routes.

1 Start with a square, white side upward. Fold in half from left to right.
2 Fold the top edge in half, marking the halfway point.
3 Take the folded edge to the pinch-mark, crease, and unfold.
4 Fold the corner over at 45 degrees, starting at the same pinchmark. Crease and unfold.
5 Make an inside-reverse fold using the most recent crease.
6 Fold the two corners on the left to meet the vertical crease (see diagram 7 for guidance).
7 Swing the upper layer to the left, carefully squashing the small triangle at the top.
8 Fold the top left corner over to the vertical center.
9 Make a crease to line up with the lower edge of the flap folded over in step 8.

The curved option

10 Fold the top right corner over between the two locations shown on page 66. Tuck it under the layer of paper.
11 Refold the lower flap upward.
12 Gently curl the paper toward you on either side.
13 Turn over for the completed variation.

The straight option

14 Turn the paper around to make the following steps easier. Fold the lower left corner over to meet a colored edge.
15 Fold over along the upper edge that you folded in step 10.
16 Using existing creases, form two right-angled corners to make the model three-dimensional.
17 The completed variation is shown onn page 66.

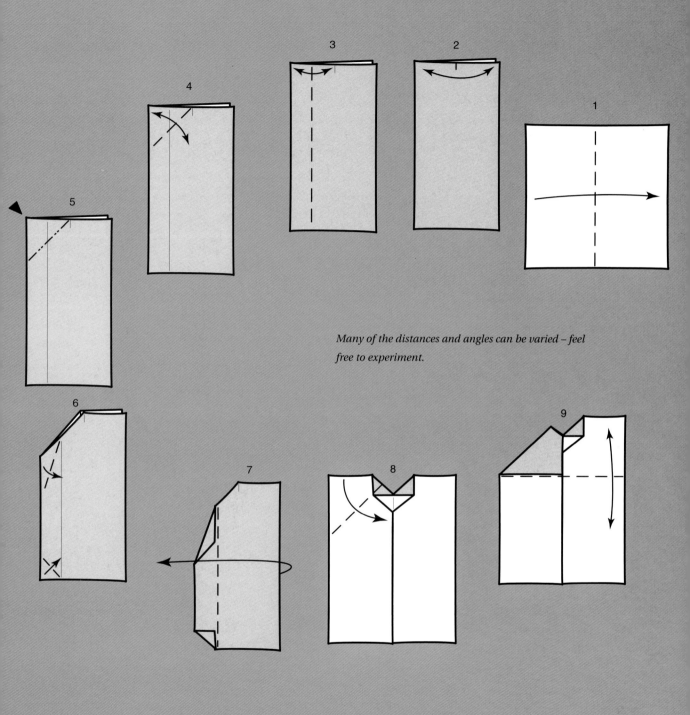

Many of the distances and angles can be varied – feel free to experiment.

Continued next page

Mountains continued

*You can continue the design along two
different paths. Try them both and
compare them.*

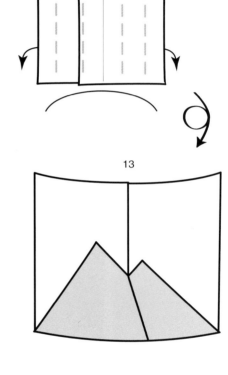

12

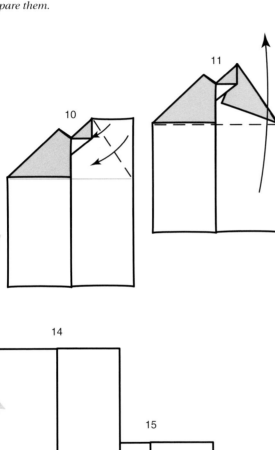

10

11

13

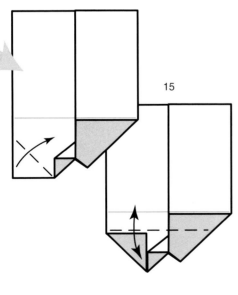

14

15

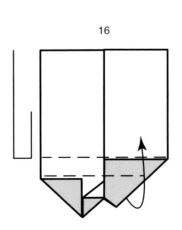

16

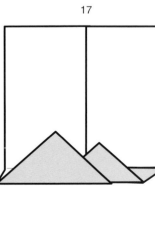

17

The Locked Glider

Design by Nick Robinson

I have written several books on paper airplanes and each time it gets harder to come up with original designs. One area well worth investigating is that of airplanes that have their front end "locked." The paper used for this lock has the bonus of concentrating weight at the front, which is generally where it needs to be. The trick is not having so many layers of paper that it becomes impossible to crease.

1 Start with a sheet of A4, creased in half. Fold each half of a short side to lie along the halfway crease.

2 Take the folded edges to meet the central crease, crease firmly, and unfold.

3 Starting at the lower end of the most recent crease, fold the raw edge to meet the crease. Repeat on the other side.

4 Refold along the creases made in step 2.

5 Take the outside folded edges to the center, but only crease through the single layer of paper.

6 Fold the tip behind, making your fold pass through the point where the most recent crease meets the folded edge.

7 Turn the paper over and fold the sharp point back to the base of the triangular section.

8 Carefully fold the plane in half.

9 Make a crease that lies along a hidden edge (in other words, inside the plane). You can easily feel where this is.

10 Open the plane a little and make an inside-reverse fold using the crease you have just made.

11 As you fold the sides of the plane together, tuck the flap under a layer to hold it in place.

12 Open the wings out to a slight upward angle to make the completed model.

Continued next page

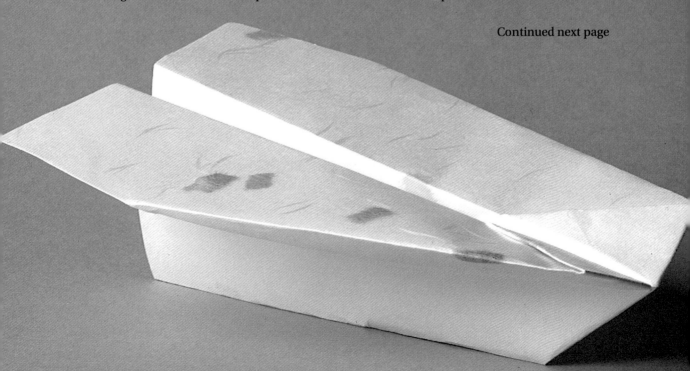

The Locked Glider continued

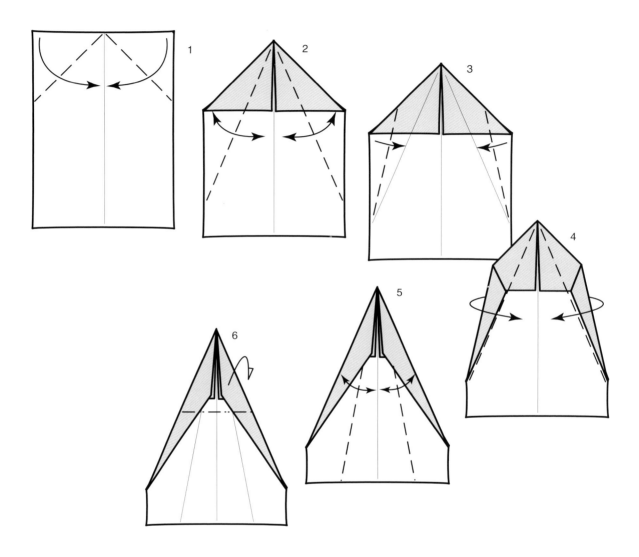

*Paper airplanes are both fun to fold and fly. There are
many specialist books on the subject.*

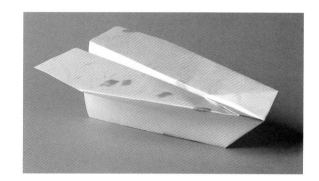

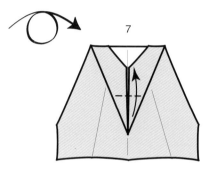

7

8

9

10

Creative challenge

When you launch a paper plane, there are three things to consider: the speed at which you launch it, the angle at which you launch it (this varies from straight in front to straight up), and finally the angle of the wings relative to the body. Each of these will have an effect on the flight characteristics. Alter one of them and see what effect it has. Only when you have all three correct will the plane fly to the best of its ability.

11

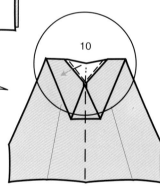

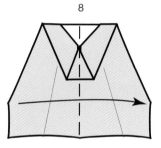

12

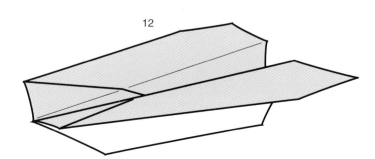

69

Butterfly

Design by Nick Robinson

Butterflies are a very popular subject in origami, because they can be simplified to a high degree yet still remain recognizable. In addition, they make good use of brightly colored paper and are perfect for displaying. This design takes elements from a traditional Frog base, but utilizes the extra paper of an A4 sheet to create large wings.

1   Start with a sheet of A4, or similar rectangle. Fold the two short edges together.

2   Make two short creases by taking the raw edge to the folded edge (it is easier than the other way round – try it and see). Open the paper out.

3   Rotate the paper through 90 degrees. Fold in half the "other" way.

4   Fold the left-hand lower edge up to meet the vertical crease. Turn the paper over and repeat on the other side. (I have drawn this second fold as a mountain fold, which saves me from drawing an extra diagram.)

5   Put your fingers into the inner pocket and open the sides out, flattening on the other axis. It sounds difficult, but is actually quite easy.

6   This shows a few pre-creases that will make life easier later on. Fold the lower edge to the crease and unfold again.

7   Fold the vertical raw edges to the same crease, but extend the crease only halfway down.

8   Squash-fold the lower edge on the existing creases.

9   Fold each raw edge inward, tucking the paper under the triangular flap. Repeat the last sequence of folds on the other side.

10 This is the result. Fold the small triangular flap backward and forward.

11 Now sink the flap inside.

12 Fold the lower edge to the center crease.

13 Fold the corner out, starting at the left-hand corner and extending the crease down to the very center of the paper. Make this crease, and then undo steps 11 and 12.

14 Reverse fold the paper inward then partially back out again, using the crease made in steps 12 and 13. This technique is known as a "crimp." Repeat on the other wing.

15 Fold both wings down along the line of the folded edge.

16 Fold them back up again, starting at the center, at a slight angle.

17 This should be the result.

18 Fold the upper layer over, allowing the layer underneath (which joins it) to stretch into a new position. The end result should look neat and, after a few attempts, it will.

19 Pull out the pocket from underneath and tuck the flap into it.

20 Repeat the last two steps on the other wing.

21 The completed butterfly.

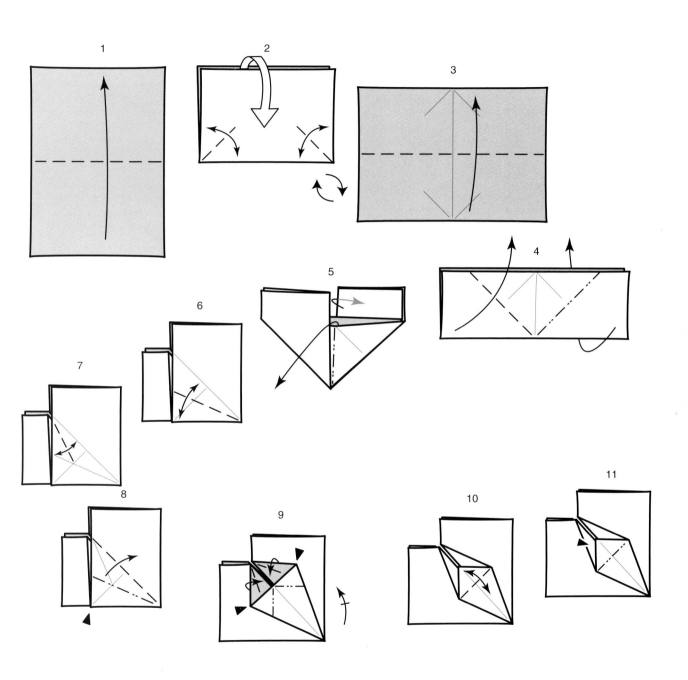

Continued next page

Butterfly continued

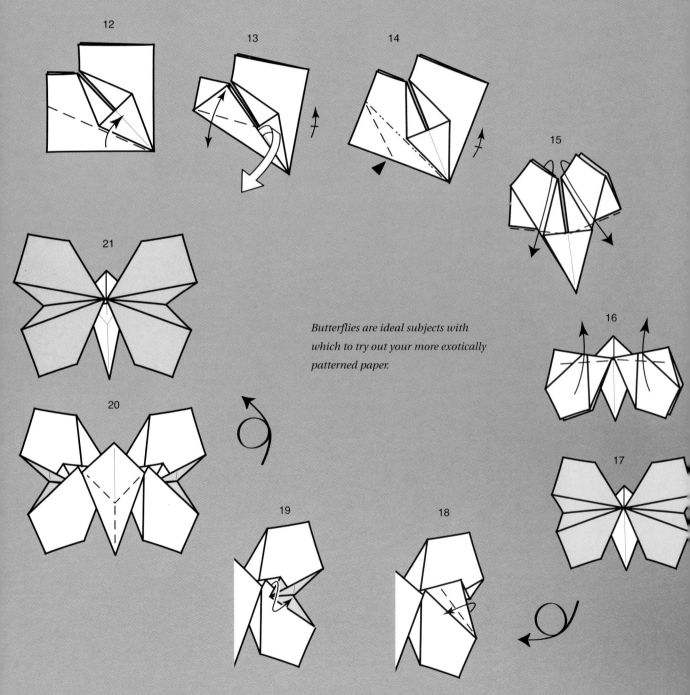

Butterflies are ideal subjects with which to try out your more exotically patterned paper.

Creative challenge

What happens if you make the rectangle
slightly longer or wider? Can you make this
model from a square?

Practical Folds

MOST PEOPLE THINK of origami as a decorative art and that the beautiful things you make from paper should be put on display. However, there is also a functional side to origami: you can make envelopes, containers, dishes, trays, cups, wallets, hats, and a whole host of other useful and practical folds. If a fold is to be handled repeatedly, you'll need to choose a paper that can cope with the stresses and strains of everyday use. You'll also need to select the correct size of paper so that the finished design is the right size for the use to which you wish to put it.

You might think that designing origami for practical use would inhibit the range of creative options open to you, but this isn't the case. There are, for example, probably more origami containers and boxes than any other type of object. Each of them is subtly or distinctly different from the others. In the northwest of England there is even a small group of folders known as the British Origami Container Society, who specialize in this area.

Although it is tempting to concentrate only on the functional aspect of the design when you are making practical folds, it is just as important to consider the folding sequence and the visual effect. People will usually take no notice of an ugly container, no matter how practical it may be. Always strive to achieve your result with the minimum of creases and try to produce elegant solutions to design problems.

Popcorn/Chip Bag

Design by Nick Robinson

Paper is perfectly suited to making quick and easy containers of all kinds. Here is one you can use to store candy, popcorn, chips, and many other things! It makes use of the creases for the Diamond Base.

1   Start with a square, colored side downward. Fold in half from one corner to the opposite corner, to form a diagonal.
2   Fold one side to the central crease.
3   Fold the flap over once more, using the original diagonal crease.
4   Turn the paper over and repeat step 2.
5   Fold the colored triangular section over the white flap, crease, and unfold.
6   Unfold the white flap.
7   Refold the triangular section to the right.
8   Tuck the loose flap carefully into the pocket of the triangular section.
9   Fold the sharp corner to the opposite corner, crease, and unfold.
10 Fold on the same crease, but tuck the point inside the pocket.
11 Turn the paper around and open the pocket at the longest edge.

Helpful hint

At step 10, you can unfold to step 7 and form an inside-reverse fold by altering some of the creases as shown. The loose white corner can be tucked into a narrow triangular pocket. This locks the paper securely in place and the whole section can now be carefully tucked into the colored triangular pocket. Although this is a slightly more difficult sequence, it makes the bag even less likely to unfold when it is full!

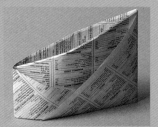

You can quickly make this design from a sheet of newspaper.

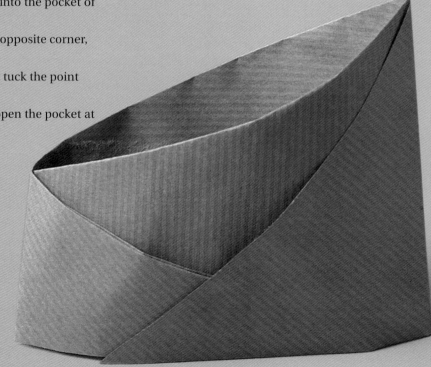

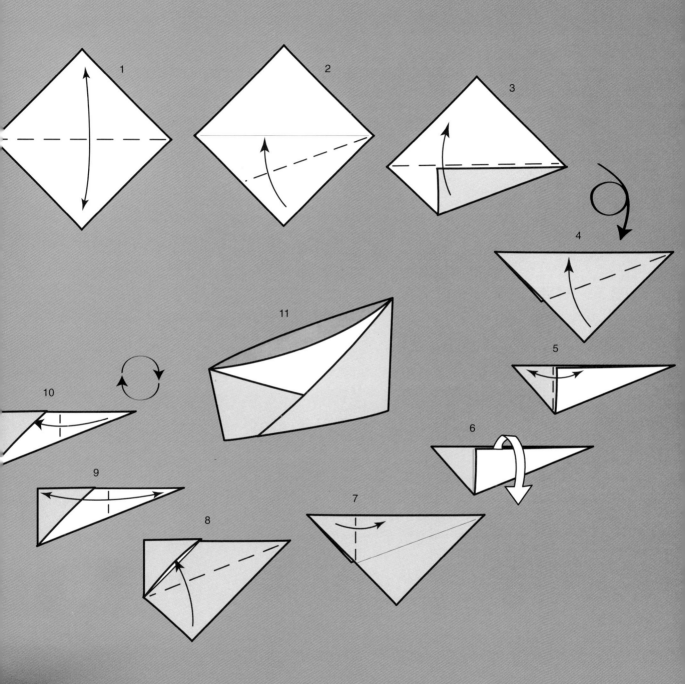

Can you create a similar design?

Wallet

Design by Nick Robinson

It is always useful to be able to make wallets of any kind. Some wallets have a slightly more complicated folding sequence with many different pockets, but this one has a pocket on each side and is perfect for stamps, credit cards, and so forth. You'll need a square of paper with sides just over four times as long as the longest side of the cards you intend to store. If you're going to keep the wallet in your pocket, you'll need paper that can withstand the wear and tear.

1   Start with a square that has been folded in half both ways. Fold the lowest edge to the center, crease, and unfold.

2   Fold both lower corners to the center, crease, and unfold.

3   Fold both lower corners to the nearest intersection of creases. Fold the upper edge to the center.

4   Fold each half of the lower raw edge to meet the nearest crease.

5   Refold the lower flaps on existing creases.

6   This is the result. Turn the paper over.

7   Fold the left- and right-hand edges to the vertical center crease.

8   Fold the upper section over on an existing crease.

9   Open the "pocket" slightly and tuck the lower triangle into it.

10 Turn over for the completed wallet.

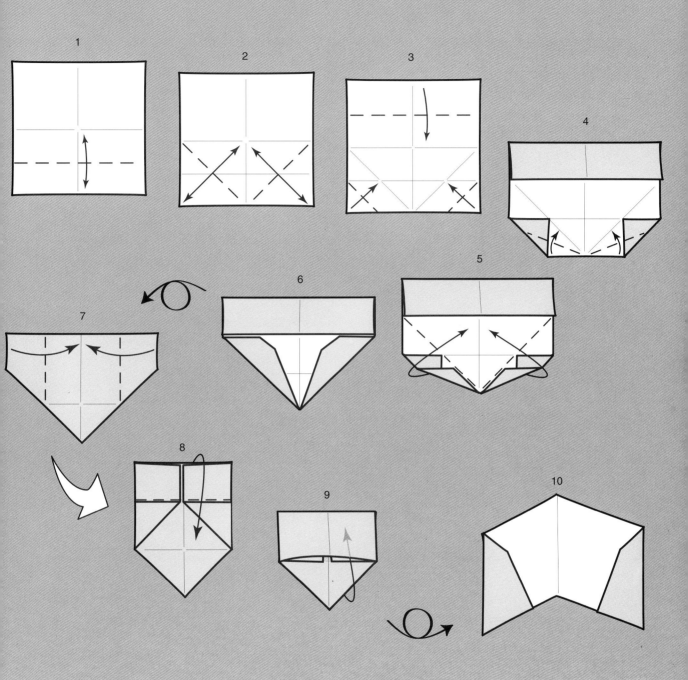

Creative challenge

The angle change achieved in step 4 is purely for decorative purposes. Can you work out how to fold the paper so that the pocket runs from the bottom center of the wallet to the outer corners?

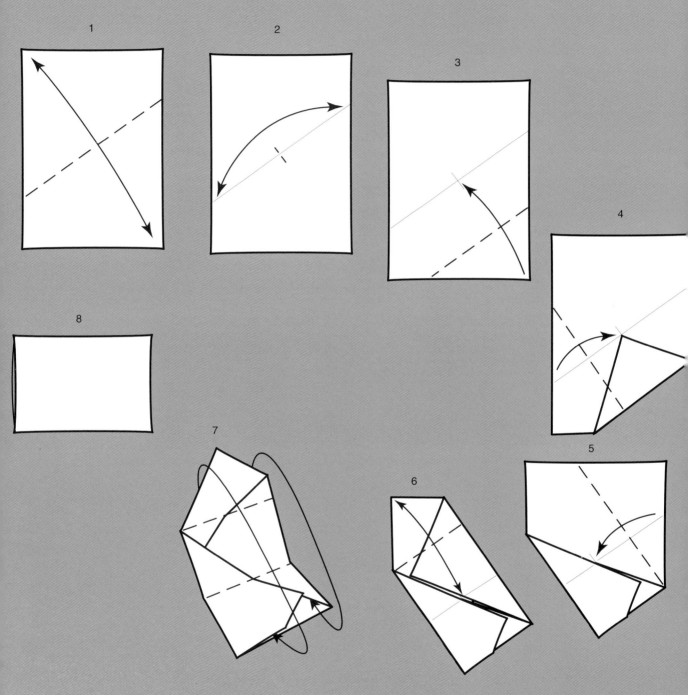

Envelopes are a great place to start creating your own designs. Make sure they can be easily read without unfolding.

Daisy's envelope

Design by Nick Robinson

There is a small society devoted to envelopes called ELFA (Envelope and Letter-folding Association). Envelopes are a wonderful challenge to paper-folders. The aim is simple: to fold a letter in such a way that it can be posted like an envelope and won't easily come undone. This allows you a wide range of creative options, although, as ever, simple, elegant designs are the aim of most creative folders. This design couldn't be much simpler, yet it holds together extremely well.

1 Start with a sheet of A4, or similar rectangle. Fold the bottom right corner to meet the top left, crease, and unfold.

2 Fold one end of this crease to the other and make a small pinch-mark to locate the center of the line.

3 Fold the bottom right corner to the center.

4 Fold the left-hand end of the crease to the center.

5 Repeat with the right-hand end of the crease.

6 Fold the top left corner to the center, crease, and unfold.

7 Fold along the first crease you made, tucking the top flap into two pockets of the bottom flap, one at either end.

8 The completed envelope.

Creative challenge

Can you create your own envelope? It should be secure so that the contents can't easily be read without unfolding and should withstand the rigors of the postal service. If so, please send me a letter using it, addressed c/o the publishers.

BOS membership secretary
2a The Chestnuts
Countesthorpe
Leicester
LE8 5TL
England

Paulo's Dish

Design by Nick Robinson

Throughout my creative origami life, I keep returning to dishes. My aim is to create the ultimate simple dish, which holds its shape using the tension of the paper and nothing else. This design is the closest I have come to reaching that goal and I currently cannot think of a simple "lock." The design is named after, and dedicated to, my good friend Paulo Mulatinho, who has done so much to promote the appreciation of elegant and beautiful origami.

1 Start with a square, white side upward. Crease both diagonals.

2 Fold the lower right side to lie along the horizontal diagonal. Crease only from the vertical diagonal back to where an imaginary halfway crease would meet it.

3 Rotate the paper 90 degrees clockwise and repeat. Each time you add a crease, it forms a location for the next one. Repeat on all four sides. Then repeat the same steps 1–3, folding in the opposite direction.

4 The result should be an octagonal crease pattern in the center of the paper. Ideally, the creases should extend no farther than necessary, but you can improve on them each time you fold the design.

5 Fold in half along a diagonal.

6 Fold the bottom corner to meet the intersection of creases, crease and unfold. Repeat on the other corner, from the other side. Open the paper and make the same two folds along the other diagonal.

7 Open the paper and begin to form it into a three-dimensional shape by pinching the corners together.

8 Looking from the side, fold two layers over at the corner on an existing crease.

9 Fold the triangular flap over and press the paper flat through all the layers. Repeat on the three remaining corners.

10 Using your fingers and thumbs, encourage the dish into a circular shape.

11 The completed dish.

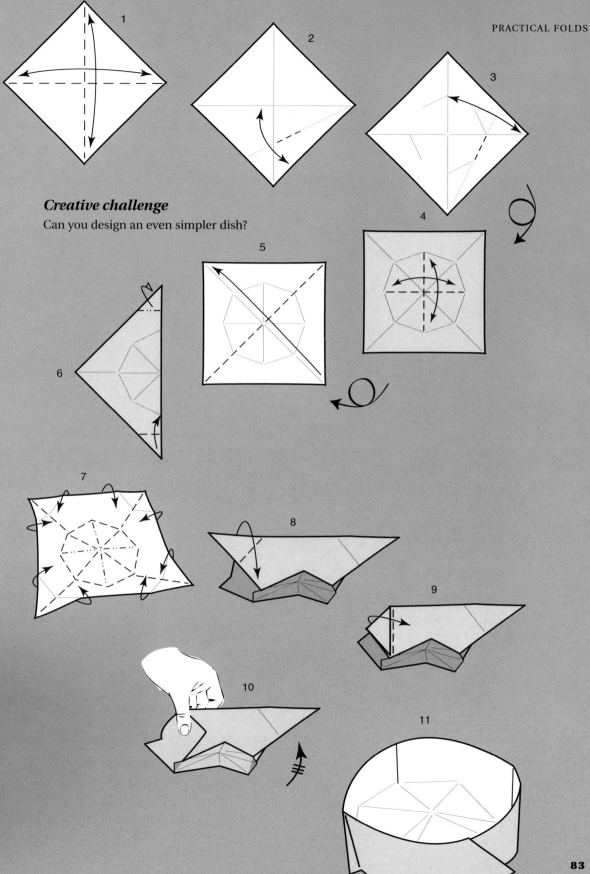

Creative challenge

Can you design an even simpler dish?

CD Cover

Design by Nick Robinson

This design is a great opportunity to practice pre-creasing. The technique involves making a number of precisely located creases, unfolding each time, and using the creases later in the sequence to create the model itself.

1   Start with a sheet of A4 and fold it in half, long edge to long edge. Crease and unfold.

2   Crease the quarter marks.

3   Fold each outside corner to the farthest quarter mark. These creases extend all the way.

4   Fold each outside corner to the crease made in step 3. These creases extend all the way.

5   Fold the lower edge to the vertical center crease, creasing only where shown. Repeat on the other side.

6   Fold one end of the most recent crease to the opposite end. Crease lightly where this fold passes through the center crease.

7   Fold the lower raw edge to touch the crease made in step 6. Crease and unfold.

8   Fold the lower raw edge to touch the ends of the crease made in step 5 and fold over on the crease made in step 7.

9   Crease and unfold where shown.

10 Swivel the paper inside on both sides. These creases are already in place.

11 This is the result.

12 Now you must work on the other end of the paper. Fold the two corners in to lie along the existing creases.

13 Fold the sides in along the existing creases.

14 Pull the paper out and allow the side flaps to tuck underneath on either side.

15 Insert the CD and fold the top edge down, tucking it into the pocket.

16 The completed CD cover.

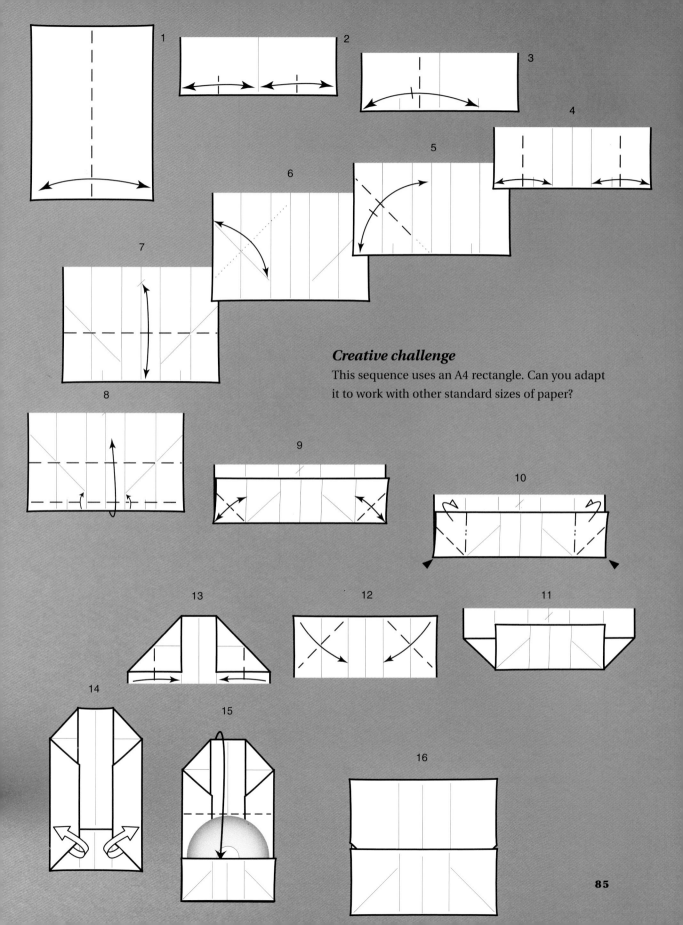

Creative challenge

This sequence uses an A4 rectangle. Can you adapt it to work with other standard sizes of paper?

Container

Design by Nick Robinson

Boxes and containers are a favorite subject for creators. If you can find a technique that gives one raised side and apply it to the other three sides, you have some sort of container! Containers are highly practical as well as decorative. This design combines two bases, the Blintz and the Multiform. The blintzed flaps are used to lock together the sides of the container.

1 Start with a square. Crease both diagonals from the white side and fold four corners to the center to form a Blintz base.

2 Fold the corners to the center again and turn the paper over.

3 Fold the "new" corners to the center again, crease, and unfold, including the creases made in step 2.

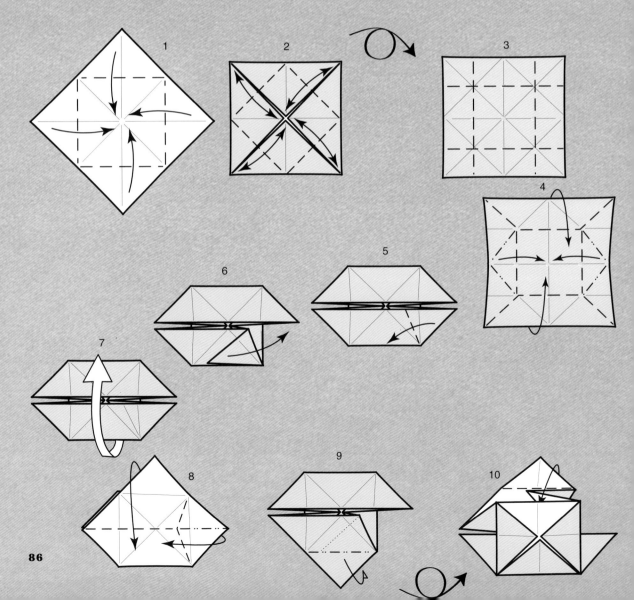

4 Use the creases shown to fold the Multiform base.

5 Fold the lower right side to lie along the lower edge.

6 Unfold again.

7 Pull the original corner out from underneath and fold it all the way up.

8 Reform the creases as shown, to make an inside-reverse fold. (The inside edge is indicated by a dotted line.)

9 Tuck the lower flap into the pocket underneath.

10 This shows step 8 seen from below. The single layer of paper tucks into the pocket, trapping the layers together.

11 Fold the two flaps in opposite directions and rotate the paper through 90 degrees.

12 The corner is now locked in place. Repeat the sequence from step 5 on the remaining three corners.

13 This is the result after all four sides have been folded. You can now open the layers from the center and shape the final container.

14 The completed container.

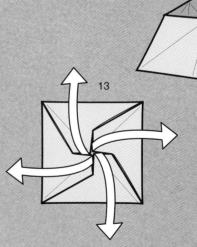

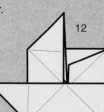

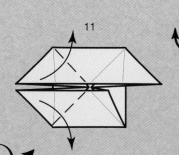

Creative challenge

Look carefully at the angle formed by the crease in step 5. Is it possible to form a square container by folding the flap in at 90 degrees, using an existing crease rather than folding this one? If not, what other angles would work?

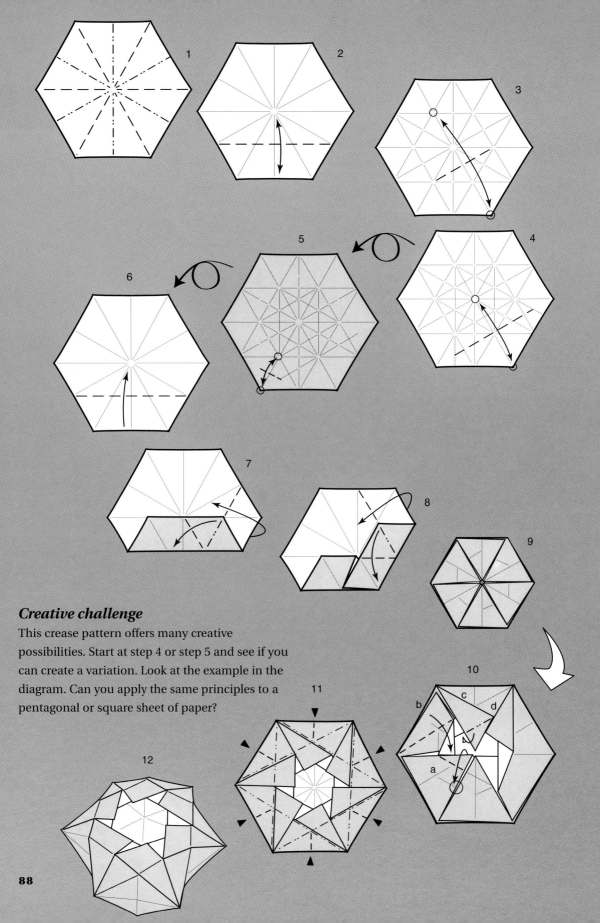

Creative challenge

This crease pattern offers many creative possibilities. Start at step 4 or step 5 and see if you can create a variation. Look at the example in the diagram. Can you apply the same principles to a pentagonal or square sheet of paper?

88

Star Dish

Design by Francis Ow

A hexagonal sheet of paper offers many possibilities for creating dishes and containers. In addition, the 60-degree geometry results in beautiful crease patterns and a very natural feel to the folding sequences. Francis Ow of Singapore is a geometric folder of great talent who has produced many exciting and original designs.

1   Start with a large hexagon, with all the "fold-in-half" type creases present, in the direction shown.
2   Fold one side to the center, crease, and unfold. Repeat with the other sides.
3   Fold a corner to the opposite inside corner of the star crease pattern. Crease only within the central hexagon shape. Repeat on the other corners.
4   Fold a corner to the center, but only crease as far as the dotted lines. This is in order to leave the exposed paper of the final form as clean as possible.

5   Turn the paper over and fold the corner to the nearest intersection. Only crease the section shown.
6   Now you can begin the assembly. This diagram shows much of the crease pattern removed to make the sequence clearer. Fold in one of the sides.
7   Use one of the creases shown to form a triangular "Rabbit's Ear" flap that flattens to the left.
8   This is the result. Repeat on the remaining sides. You will need to open the first one slightly to allow the final flap to fall into place.
9   This is the result.
10   Look carefully at this diagram. It shows a sequence of three steps and the fourth (finished) stage. Each step should be carried out on all six sides before starting the next step.
a)   Fold an inside corner back to meet the crease. Lift the flap on the right to make this easier.
b)   Swing the triangular point over to the center.
c)   Fold the tip of the point behind the white (folded) edge.
d)   This is how each of the six sections should look when complete.
11   Make sure all the central layers are firmly flattened into place, and start to form the paper gently into a three-dimensional shape by pressing in the center of each side. Put your fingers inside the dish to help create the shape. Use the minimum effort required or the model may crumple.
12   The finished dish.

Decorative Folds

THE DESIGNS IN this chapter don't necessarily seek to "look like" something. The aim, as favored by designers of complex folds, is to represent the subject as a whole and incorporate as many of its aspects as technique and approach allow. Some designers simplify the subject and try to capture its essence in a few carefully thought-through creases. A further, much smaller group of folders, looks at the subject from a different perspective; they seek to present a stylized, even spiritual, representation of the chosen subject.

The point I'm laboring to make is that it doesn't matter if your horse has three legs, your butterfly has no legs, or your octopus has six legs. Your folds can be flat or three-dimensional. They can be realistic or abstract. What matters is that you strive to make a statement and communicate it through the paper. Aim to capture the life within the subject and fold it in such a way that it represents your own vision. If you succeed, your work will be instantly recognized, since it will reflect your personality and tastes. If your folding lacks "life," it will never be truly great no matter how simple, complex, or realistic it may be.

Gone Fishing

Design by Nick Robinson

This model falls into the "spiritual" category. The bird and the fish (hunter and hunted) are made abstract to represent a narrative about the cycle of life. I call this approach "painting with paper." The techniques involved are almost irrelevant compared with the way in which the color contrasts of the paper depict the subject.

1   Start with a large square, colored side upward. Fold in half from left to right.
2   Fold over the first layer of the bottom right-hand corner. See diagram 3 for guidance.
3   This diagram focuses on the lower end of the paper. Make an asymmetrical pleat to form the fish's fin.
4   Tuck the lower raw edge of the flap behind the fin, and fold over the layer from underneath.
5   Form the lower fin with an off-center Rabbit's Ear, adjusting it until it matches diagram 6.
6   Fold the end of the fish over, opening and squashing the paper to form a tail. The exact position of the crease is not important.
7   Swing the upper layer of the fish back out again, undoing the tail folds.
8   Mountain-fold the top layer in between the layers to hide a raw edge. Re-form the lower half of the fish
9   Now you must work on the other end of the paper. Fold over a small flap.
10 Fold over a larger flap, at an angle.
11 Fold over both flaps on a crease that joins the two corners.
12 Fold the first layer back down.
13 Narrow the point by about one-third.
14 Fold the lower section down.
15 Tuck the paper into the pocket underneath.
16 Make a small pleat to form the eye.
17 The completed model.

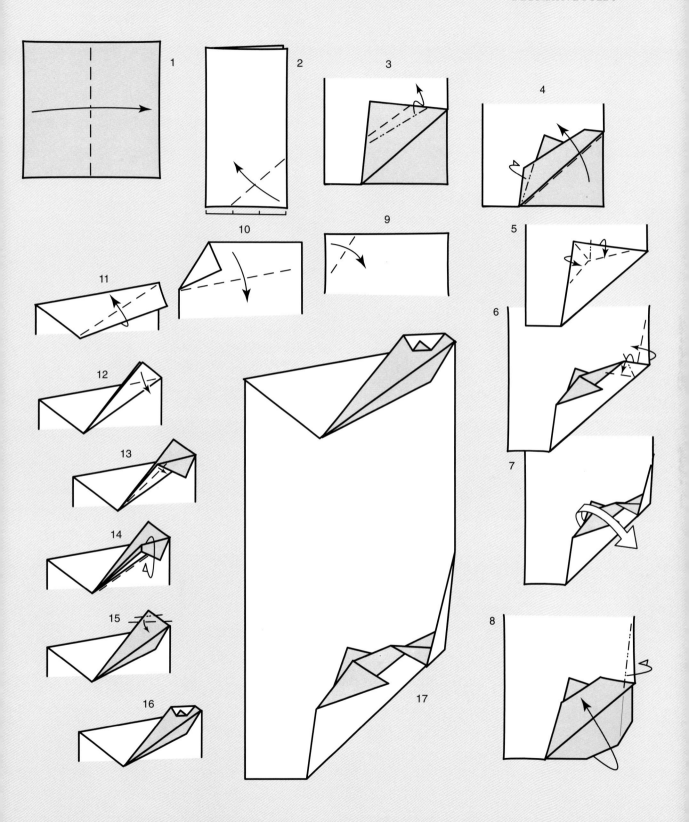

Escher Fish Tessellation

Design by Nick Robinson

*Tessellations are shapes that fit together to form a
continuous surface. Origami is well suited to
producing both simple and sometimes more
complex tessellations. This one is based on the work
of Maurits Escher and is inspired by a design of the
Briton, Mick Guy. When finished, the fish appear to
swim in opposite directions, yet merge together.*

1   Start with a Preliminary base, white side out,
which has been unfolded back to the square.
Fold one corner to the center.

2   Re-form the Preliminary base.

3   Fold the first layer on the left across to
the right.

4   Fold the lower corner to the opposite corner.

5   Fold back two layers to form the mirror image
of step 3.

6   Fold the corner upward again.

7   Fold back a single layer.

8   Fold the upper sides of the
square shape to meet
the vertical
center crease.

9   Pull out the
hidden layers (see
diagram 10 for guidance).

10   Fold the lower corner up,
making a crease that joins the two
existing creases.

11   Swivel the left-hand side over to the right,
using the existing creases.

12   Mountain-fold the flap behind on a
vertical crease.

13   Repeat step 11 on the right-hand side.

14   Fold the flap behind as before, to form the
completed fish.

Helpful hint

By rearranging the layers, you can make the two
sides of the fish hold together more securely. These
are the steps to follow.

15   At step 12, unfold the left-hand flap back to
step 11 and unfold the original corner on the
right-hand side.

16   Fold the right-hand flap over using the
creases shown.

17   Fold the lower corner to meet the upper
corner, flattening the paper into a shape
similar to a Fish Base.

18   Swing the white half-Kite-shaped
section underneath.

19   Refold the left-hand section as with
the original design, tucking the flap
into the pocket you
have just made.

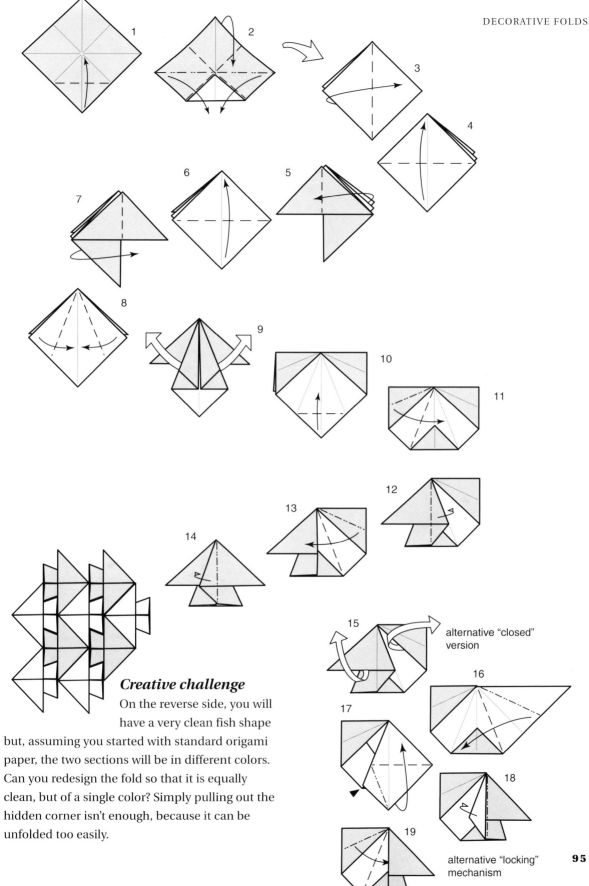

Creative challenge

On the reverse side, you will have a very clean fish shape but, assuming you started with standard origami paper, the two sections will be in different colors. Can you redesign the fold so that it is equally clean, but of a single color? Simply pulling out the hidden corner isn't enough, because it can be unfolded too easily.

alternative "closed" version

alternative "locking" mechanism

95

Kite

Design by Nick Robinson

This is another example of "painting with paper."
Most of the creases in this design can be varied:
simply fold them to where you think they should be!
The fold itself came together very quickly once I had
"seen" the kite itself form at the corner of the paper.
The "string" was a bonus that I hadn't anticipated!

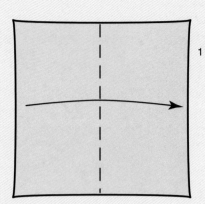

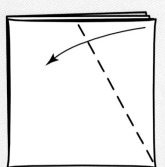

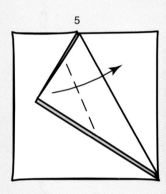

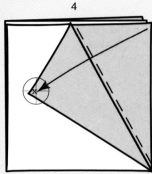

1 Start with a square, colored side upward. Fold it in half from left to right.

2 Fold it in half from bottom to top.

3 Fold a single layer over at exactly 30 degrees to the vertical. No, let's be generous. Give or take 5 degrees!

4 Fold the next layer over but not quite as far. This will create the kite's string.

5 Fold the top layer back over, to form a wide or narrow kite, as you prefer.

6 Carefully pinch a crease to indicate the kite's crossbeam.

7 The completed model.

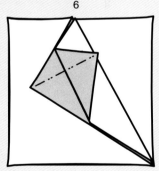

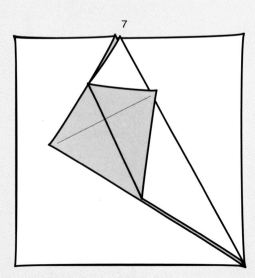

Creative challenge
Try using a rectangle to form a kite with longer string.

For a neat result, you must be very accurate, so take your time and work slowly.

A4 Rhombic Unit

Design by Nick Robinson

Origami has many examples of modular designs. An origami module usually contains pockets and flaps and should hold together without aids such as glue or sticky tape. Complex modular designs can require many hundreds of identical units, but I never have the patience to fold them. I limit myself to a few units and see what I can achieve. This unit makes use of the unique geometry of the A4 rectangle: you can cut a sheet of A4 in half and be left with two sheets of identical proportions to the original.

1   Start with a sheet of A4 with the color desired for the outside of the finished design face upward. Fold the two shorter edges together and pinch the halfway points. Unfold.

2   Fold the same short edges to meet the center creases. Make sharp creases and unfold.

3   Turn the paper over. Fold the bottom left-hand corner to meet the top center point. Make sure these two points meet exactly and crease the paper.

4   This is the result. Unfold and repeat step 3 on the three remaining corners.

5   This shows the crease pattern. Refold the bottom left-hand crease.

6   These creases are now in place. Fold following the direction of the arrow. As the flap folds using the valley crease, the left-hand upper edge of paper swings in to form a double layer. See diagram 7 for guidance.

7   Repeat step 6 on the opposite corner. It may be helpful to unfold the first corner then fold this step, before completing both corners. Part of the paper tucks underneath (see diagram 8).

8   This is the result.

9   Turn the paper over, crease (a) and fold (b) the single-layer flaps within the layers.

10   See Assembly below.

Assembly

There are many ways of joining this unit but the easiest is probably by using 12 of them. The diagram shows three units joined to form a corner: each flap will tuck into a matching pocket.

Helpful hint

You can join 6, 8, 12, 20, or 36 units by adding a crease between the narrowest points of the central rhombus. Ambitious folders can try adding the other diagonal and seeing what options are available for joining. Try folding the module from with different sized sheets.

Continued next page

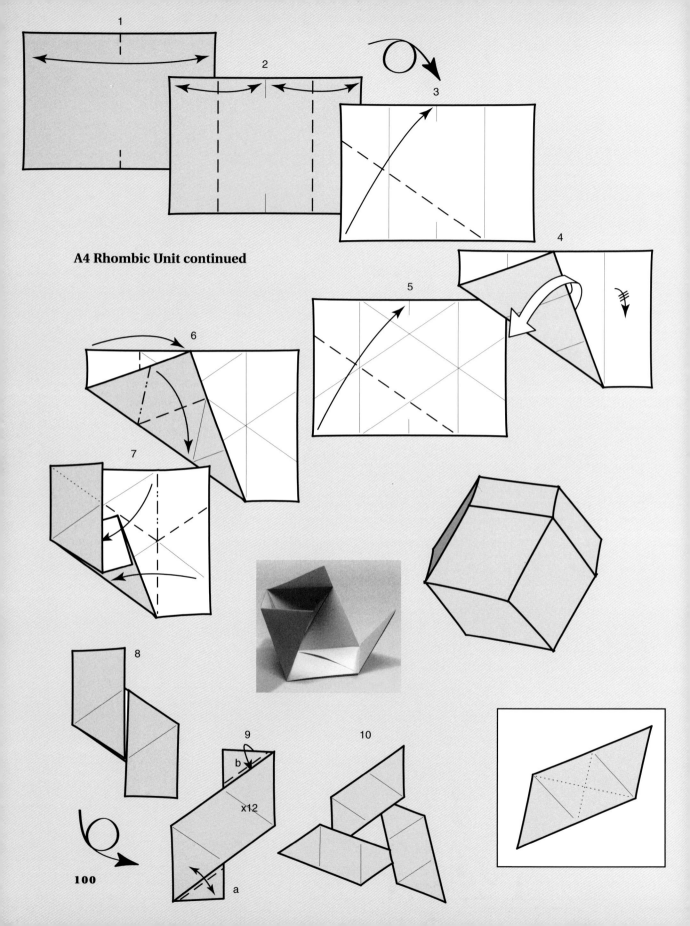

A4 Rhombic Unit continued

1

2

3

4

5

6

7

8

9

b

x12

a

10

100

LEFT: *When three units are joined the next step is to join the units to form, in this case, a rhomboid. They are joined by tucking the flaps into the corresponding pockets.*

101

Flower Form

Design by Nick Robinson

Of all my designs, this one perhaps comes closest to my idea of perfection. Although the creasing requires some concentration, it isn't difficult. Encourage the petals to curl. If you use translucent paper and have a source of light behind the model, it looks especially beautiful. There isn't much more to say about it, so fold it, sit back, and (hopefully) enjoy it. You will need to fold this several times to get it perfect.

1   Start with a square, and crease it in half both ways.

2   Fold the bottom corner to the upper-right halfway point. Crease from the halfway point to an imaginary Blintz (corner-to-center) fold.

3   Rotate the paper through 90 degrees each time, repeating step 2 on each corner.

4   Carefully crease a small central square. Fold with feeling!

5   Turn the paper over and repeat steps 2 and 3 on each corner.

6   This is the final crease pattern. Turn the paper over.

7   Start to twist the paper in an anticlockwise direction as you allow the crease to fold into place. Keep twisting – carefully – as the "star" creases meet up. Fold with feeling.

8   The completed model.

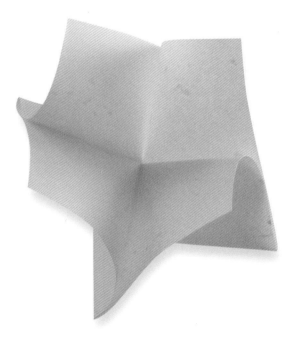

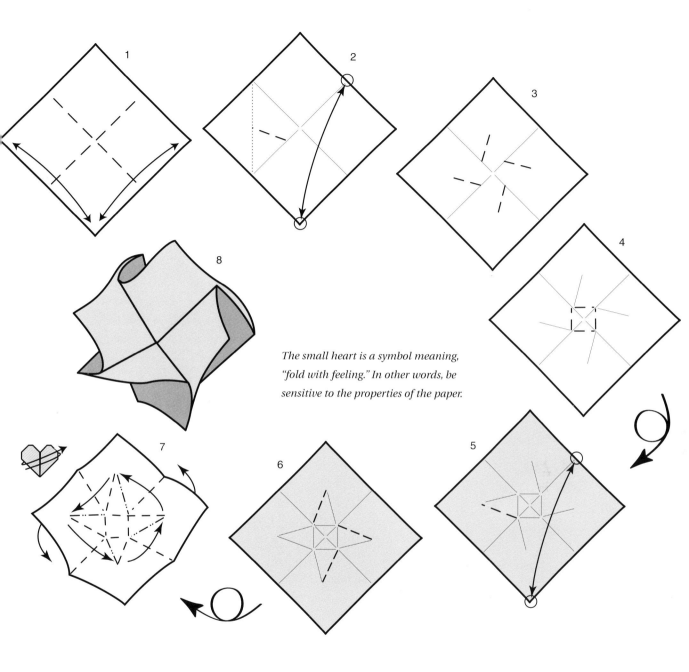

The small heart is a symbol meaning, "fold with feeling." In other words, be sensitive to the properties of the paper.

Arrow Tessellation

Design by Nick Robinson

Tessellations are shapes that can be placed together so that they form a continuous surface. Origami is well suited to producing simple tessellations and sometimes more complex ones. A seemingly ordinary shape can become spectacular when multiplied. This design was inspired by an arrow fold created by the late Dan Mason. I made several, lined them up, and suddenly saw that the arrows left arrow-shaped "holes" going in the opposite direction! These origami "visions" are often the key to creating. Remember though, you may have an idea in a fraction of a second but the finished design may take a lot longer to perfect!

1 Start with a square, white side up and crease both diagonals.

2 Fold two adjacent corners to the centre, crease and unfold.

3 Fold the corners halfway in, then roll the paper over again on the crease made in step 2.

4 Turn the paper over and fold the two original corners to meet the nearest angled corners.

5 Fold the raw edge back out to the folded edge.

6 Unfold the double layer flap.

7 Turn the paper over and fold the two corners in to meet the short raw edges.

8 This is the result. Turn the paper over.

9 Fold two corners to the center, the "cut off" corner inward and double fold the remaining corner (as in step 3).

10 Turning over will produce a single arrow "unit." Using the flaps on the underneath, you can wrap them around each other to hold the units in place. The more "wraps," the tighter the finished result.

Creative hints

These units look best if folded with great care and accuracy. They can be placed under a glass frame for an eye-catching display.

The more individual units you make, the more impressive the tesselation appears.

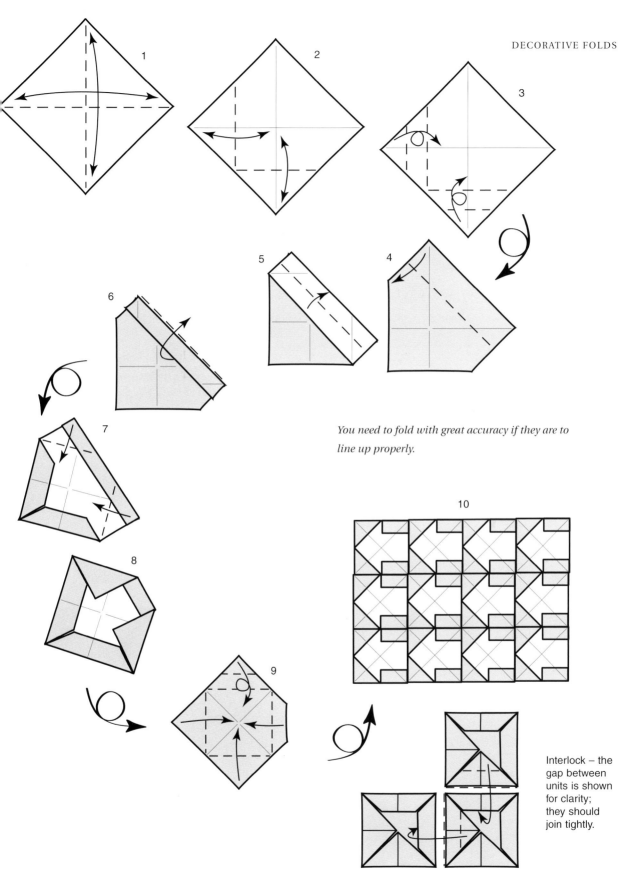

You need to fold with great accuracy if they are to line up properly.

Interlock – the gap between units is shown for clarity; they should join tightly.

Wet folding

WHEN FOLDING INANIMATE subjects, such as cars or boxes, the main aim is neatness and accuracy. When you want to fold animals or flowers, accuracy is sometimes less important than breathing life into the subject. In many origami books, the folder is encouraged to make sharp creases. The Japanese master, Akira Yoshizawa, demonstrated that some creases can be made more softly. Using his approach, a fold can possess a whole spectrum of creases, from sharp to very gentle. This offers the possibility of origami being much more expressive when it reproduces a living subject.

However, the disadvantage of gentle creases is that they don't stay in place when the fold is handled or when it is completed. The solution is wet folding: folding with dampened paper, which retains its shape when dry. The secret behind this lies in the paper's sizing. Sizing is a water-soluble adhesive that binds the fibers of the paper together and provides the stiffness. Dampening the paper dissolves the sizing, separating the fibers and leaving the paper floppy and malleable. As the paper dries, the reverse occurs, setting the fibers in the desired position.

Wet folding requires paper with the correct type of sizing. Many are simply not suitable. In general, the thicker types of paper are best, but the only true test is to try. Beware though: dampened paper is notoriously difficult to handle and tears easily. The paper also expands unevenly in the direction of the fibers, so accurate folding is also a problem. In addition, the thickness of the paper means that complex folds and a large number of layers are impossible.

I often make the first few creases then dampen the paper, trying not to wet the creases too much, as they will tear easily. To dampen the paper, use an absorbent cloth and carefully brush both sides until the sheet is uniformly damp. An alternative method is to use the fine spray from an atomizer. The key word is "damp," not "wet"! Only experience tells you how damp the paper needs to be, but if it becomes shiny when you dampen it, allow it to dry slightly before proceeding.

Since the paper dries quickly, you should fold it promptly – hence the value of knowing the folding sequence you are going to follow. Use the cloth to dampen the paper again, as and when necessary. Wet folding means that much of your folding will be performed in the air, as you continually shape and hold the paper. If I want a specific crease to dry, I blow on it. It's simple, but effective!

Once you have made your model, you can use various methods of drying it so it retains its shape. You can use a hair dryer, bright sunshine, or put the model in a draught of air.

As you will discover, the feel and appearance of wet-folded origami is impossible to achieve in any other way. The effort involved will be well worth while. Not only will you have a beautiful and sturdy fold, but it will last for many years.

Elephant

Design by Nick Robinson

This is an example of how a complex subject can be broken down into key elements – tusks, trunk, and so on. I am very fond of techniques that "trap" the paper and hold it in a three-dimensional form at the same time. The basic shape of this design is created by using just such a method in step 6. The formation of the eyes in step 15 is subtle and requires a degree of finesse. Be careful not to press too hard. You want gentle creases. As the symbol indicates, fold with feeling!

1   Start with a square creased along the diagonal. Fold two sides to the center.

2   Fold the lower point to the top.

3   Make two small pre-creases and unfold.

4   Fold the tip down to meet the inside corners.

5   Make a pre-crease to bisect the left-hand side of the triangle.

6   Open the paper out, then use the creases shown to form a three-dimensional crimp in the paper. Follow the creases carefully and don't force the paper. No extra creases are needed.

7   Repeat on the other side.

8   Turn the paper over then fold a flap back out, as shown.

9   Fold the short colored inside edge to the folded colored outside edge, crease and unfold.

10   Form a valley crease connecting the end of the last crease with the tip of the point. As you fold this over, given some encouragement, the paper should flatten neatly. See diagram 11 for guidance.

11   You enjoyed that so much, you'll want to repeat it on the other half of the same point.

12   One tusk is complete. Now repeat with the other tusk.

13   Form the head into a three-dimensional shape using the creases shown. You'll need to extend an existing crease to complete this.

14   Complete the head by folding in along existing creases (hidden creases are shown as dotted lines). This is a fun move and very elegant.

15   Finally, round the trunk and make gentle shaping folds to suggest the eyes. Try to keep the head rounded at all times and use the lightest creases you can. Fold with feeling!

16   The completed model.

Creative challenge

Can you work out how to form white tusks instead of colored ones?

Continued next page

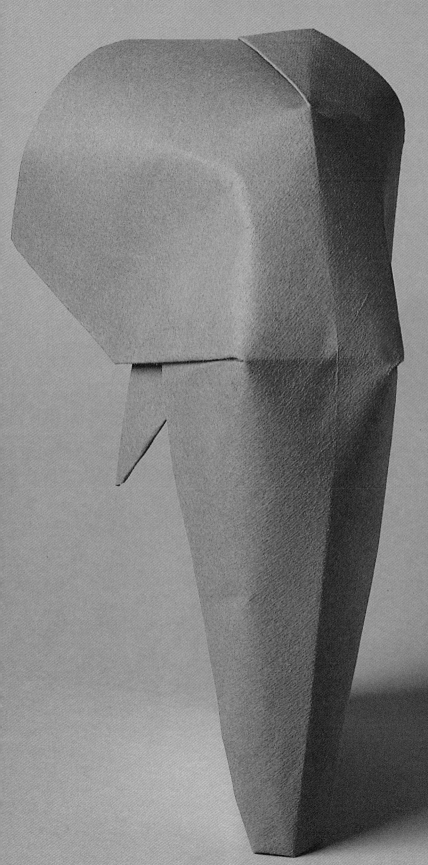

The creases forming the "eyes" need to be folded with a lot of feel for the paper. Too much pressure will result in an ugly crease.

**Elephant
continued**

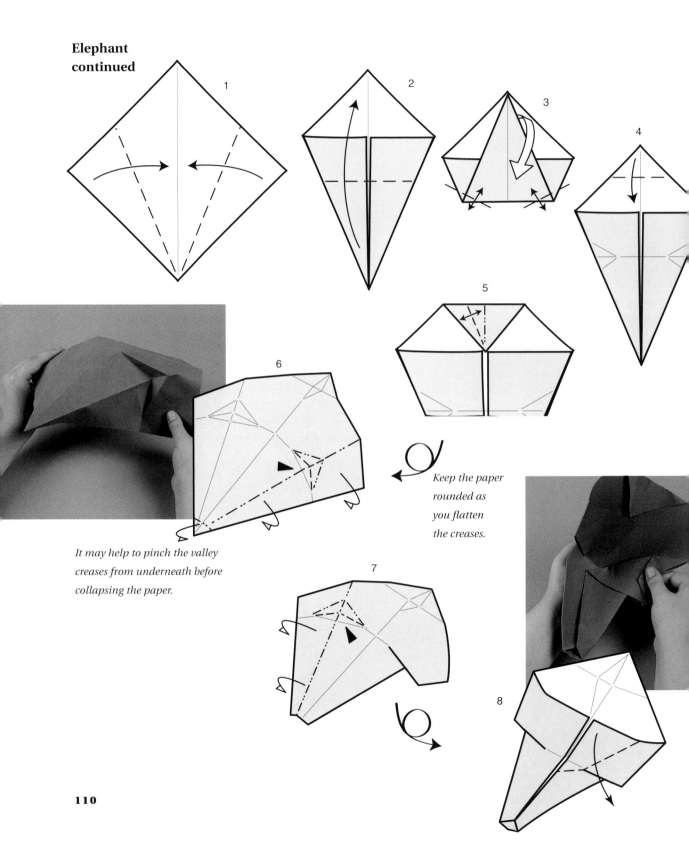

*It may help to pinch the valley
creases from underneath before
collapsing the paper.*

*Keep the paper
rounded as
you flatten
the creases.*

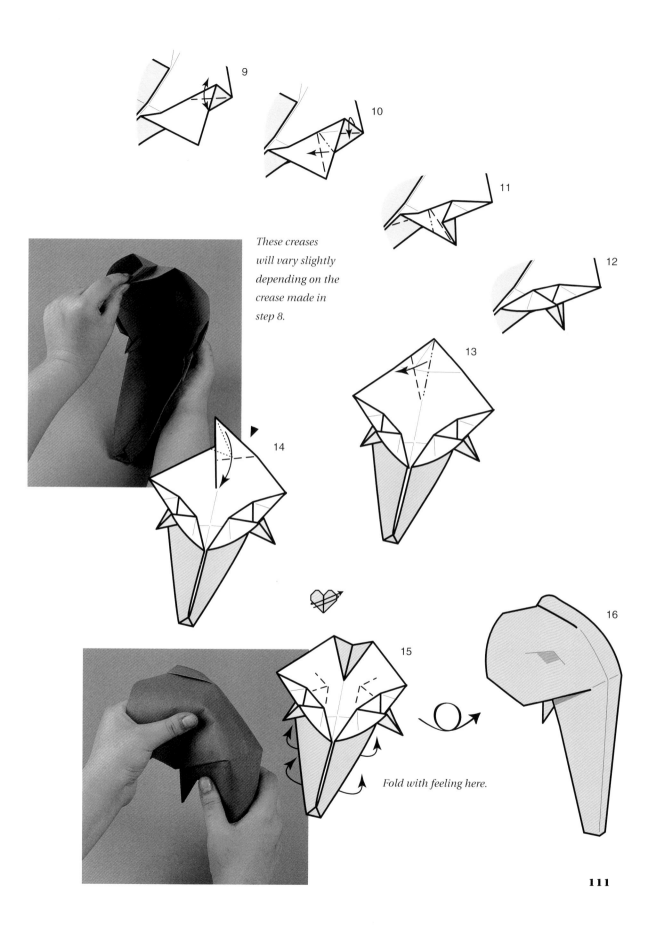

9

10

These creases will vary slightly depending on the crease made in step 8.

11

12

13

14

15

Fold with feeling here.

16

111

Baby Bird

Design by Nick Robinson

I strive to create simple designs, but also to give them some element of three-dimensionality. This design is a good example – the simple technique for forming the body almost completes the model. When I was creating this design, I had a mental image of three baby birds in their nest, beaks wide open waiting for their food.

1   Start with a square, creased along a diagonal. Fold two sides to the diagonal, crease and unfold.

2   Repeat the move with the other two sides but leave them folded.

3   This is the result. Turn the paper over.

4   Make two valley creases to lie along creases on the underside. Form the point into a Rabbit's Ear, flattened to one side. If you have got this far in the book, you shouldn't find this move too difficult.

5   Swing the point to the other side.

6   Flatten the flap symmetrically. Pre-crease the mountain fold if necessary.

7   Fold the top layer in half to the left and fold the bottom section in half to the right.

8   Make a firm crease as shown.

9   Open the paper from underneath and add two mountain creases, which allow you to give the body its three-dimensional form. It's a neat move.

10   Shape the base of the neck by emphasizing existing creases.

11   Turn over and open the beak slightly.

12   The completed model.

ABOVE: *You can clearly see how wet-folding requires you to fold in the air.*

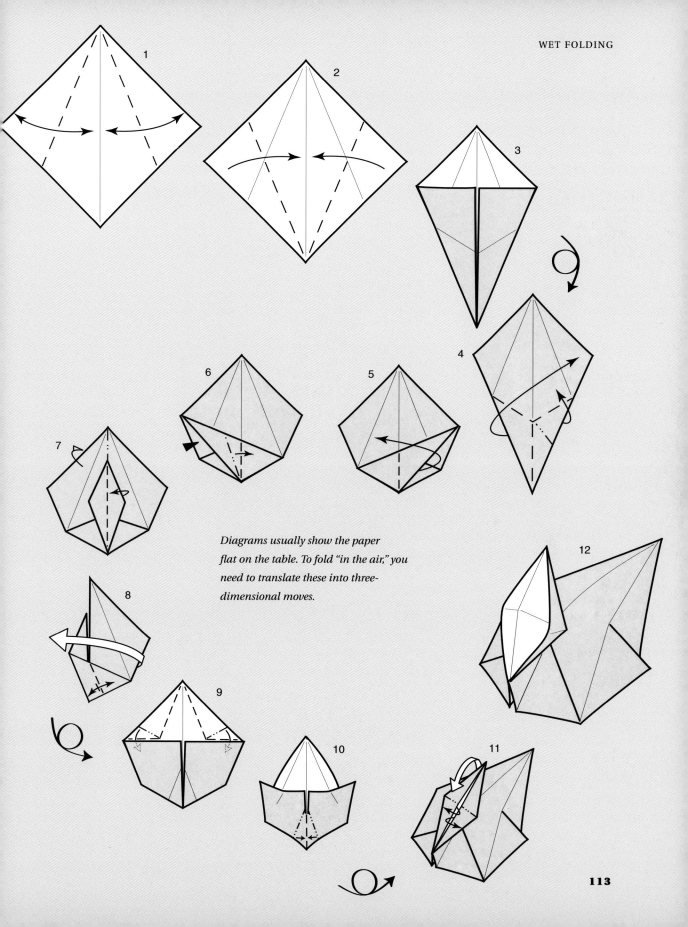

1

2

3

4

5

6

7

8

9

10

11

12

Diagrams usually show the paper flat on the table. To fold "in the air," you need to translate these into three-dimensional moves.

Horse's Head (b)

Design by David Brill

This design is taken from the version on page 50. It is a wonderful opportunity to practice your handling of the paper. It is a very simple design, yet the shaping and molding will take a lot of practice, unless you "have the gift." I recommend you use a *large sheet of paper so you can really get to grips with it. I advise you to follow the creases very carefully and to fold with feeling at all times.*

1 Start with a square folded as far as the end of step 5 on page 51.

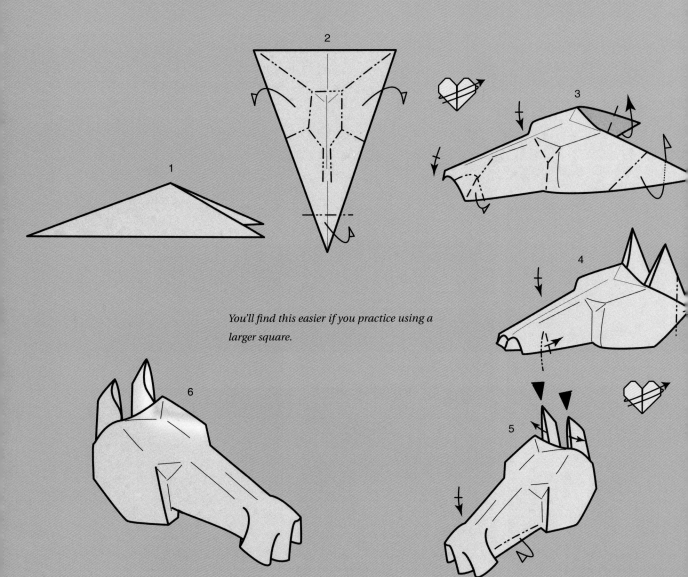

You'll find this easier if you practice using a larger square.

2 Open out back to a triangle and put in the mountain crease shown. Fold the tip of the sharp point underneath. The paper immediately becomes three-dimensional and then needs to be folded "in the air."

3 Make three light valley folds to suggest the eyes. Fold the ears inwards and upwards. Form the nostrils on either side.

4 Shape the back of the ears (easy!) and make small crimps to shape the side of the head some more.

5 Open the ears and hold the crimp in place by making a mountain fold, squashing the ends of this crease as neatly as you can.

6 The completed model. You will probably want to make this a few times!

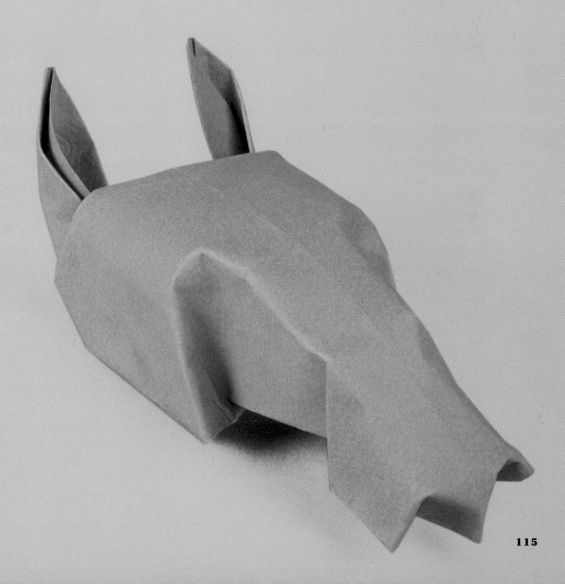

Toad

By Nick Robinson

This design uses a variation of the crease pattern for the Tree, seen earlier in this book. Several of the creases are folded "by eye" (in other words, there is no specific reference point to fold to). This means that every time you fold it, you make small adjustments from the previous time to suit your own vision of how the final model should turn out. The final step is the one that needs a careful touch; try to make it "soft" – fold with feeling!

1 Start with a square, folded in half side to side and unfolded. Fold the lower right corner to touch the crease, starting the fold at the lower left corner.

2 Like this. Unfold and repeat with the lower left corner.

3 Fold each corner to meet the other end of the crease that started at that corner. Unfold again.

4 By changing part of the creases into mountains, you can collapse the paper.

5 This is the result. Fold the left and right hand points forward. Check diagram 6 for guidance.

6 Make a valley crease through all layers.

7 Turn the paper over and make a narrow crimp fold – the paper becomes three dimensional (and stays so).

8 Fold the rear edge underneath using the crease made in step 6. The paper inside opens out neatly.

9 Here's the view from underneath. Fold the two corners inside to round the rear legs.

10 Turn over again. These final "rounding" folds are entirely up to you- the creases shown are for guidance only. Make these creases gently and try to encourage the legs to stay underneath, giving a "squat" appearance to the toad.

11 The completed toad.

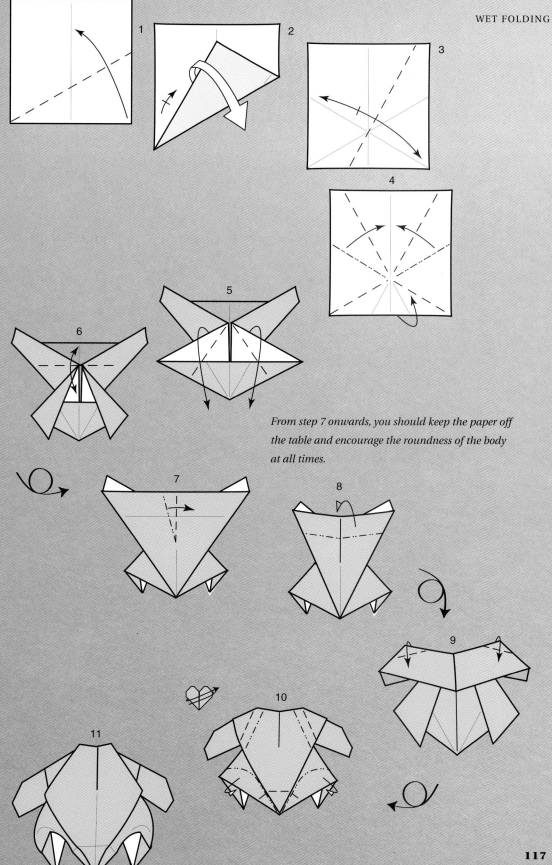

From step 7 onwards, you should keep the paper off
the table and encourage the roundness of the body
at all times.

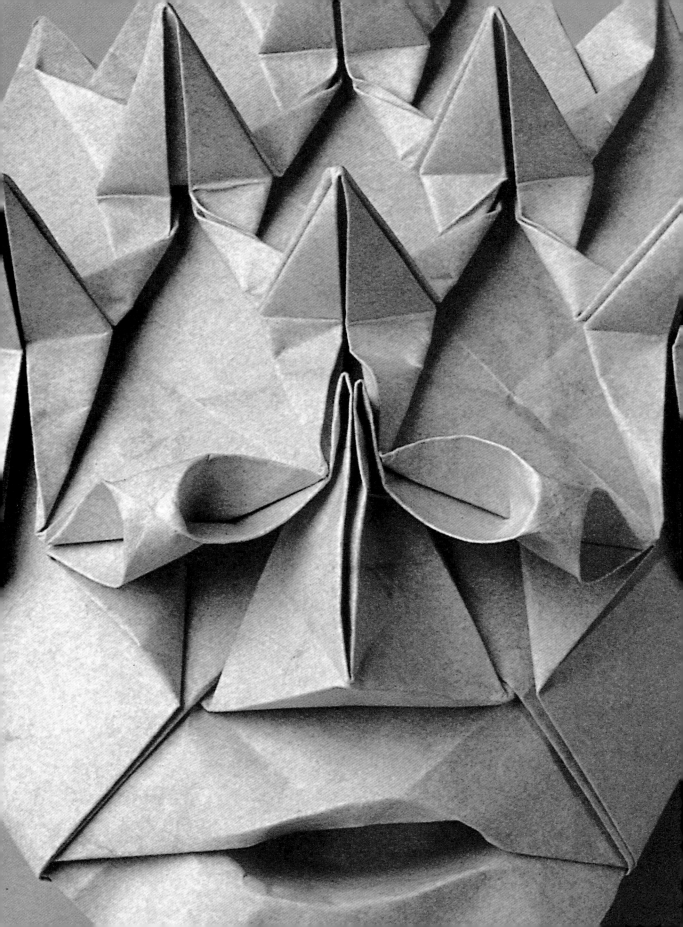

Complex Folding

ANY ART FORM has a full spectrum of complexity, ranging from the very simple to the fiendishly difficult. While individual folders will usually have a preference for a certain level of complexity, almost all folders enjoy a challenge from time to time and complex origami certainly provides that challenge. You need to be well in control of your fingers. If you make a small error at the start, it will have magnified by the time you reach the fifty-sixth step, sometimes so much so that you won't be able to finish. The old adage about practice making perfect applies to origami as to any other subject. If you start with simple folds and build up to complex ones, you should eventually be able to tackle most origami designs.

The normal guidelines for origami will serve you well for complex folding; take your time, read the text carefully, check the next few diagrams to see what you're aiming for, and start with a large sheet of paper. It may be that you don't finish the first time. Don't be disheartened, but try again in a few days. Usually, you will get a little farther each time. Folding with friends is also a good idea.

The designs in this section are far from the most complex that are available. Indeed, some would even categorize them as "intermediate." However, they are complex by my standards. Ultimately, the labels are unimportant. Just enjoy the folding.

Concorde

Design by Nick Robinson

Although Concorde itself has retired from service, its beautiful profile will never be forgotten. I've tried, in this design, to capture the lines of the plane without worrying about the fine details such as engines, undercarriage, etc. The folding sequence includes a number of useful techniques that you can employ in your own creations. The forming of the nose section requires a delicate touch, especially if you are using smaller paper.

1 Start with a square, white side upward, with a diagonal crease. Fold two adjacent sides to the center crease.

2 Fold the remaining raw edges to the crease. This forms the Diamond base.

3 Fold the bottom corner to the top corner.

4 Fold the top corner to the lower edge; make light pinch-marks only.

5 Fold the pinch-marks to the lower edge.

6 Turn the paper over.

7 Fold the tail corner to lie on the hidden edge.

8 Make a crease running from the lower right corner to the point where the right-hand side of the triangle meets the longer horizontal folded edge. Only crease as far as the center crease.

9 Repeat step 7 on the right-hand side.

10 This is difficult. Open and squash the left-hand side of the flap. The squash crease underneath uses the existing crease; the crease on the upper layer is a new crease.

11 Fold the point to the left, pulling paper out from within the flap so that both sides are identical. You might like to practice this step on a larger sheet of paper.

12 Turn the paper over.

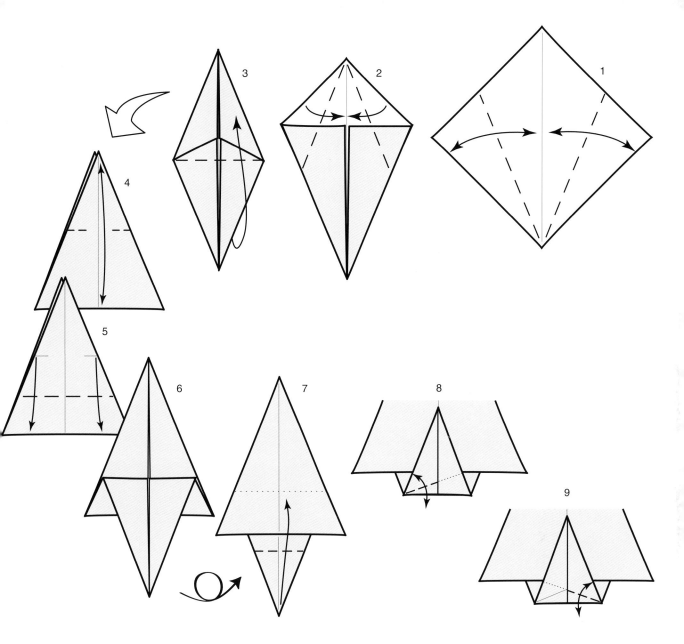

13 Fold the lower edges of the uppermost flap to the center, extending the crease as far as the upper horizontal edge. Swivel the outer edges so that the paper lies flat.

14 This is the result. Turn the paper over.

15 Starting from the tail section, make two vertical creases. Turn the paper over once more.

16 Make two more vertical creases close to the center crease. These creases end at the same place as the outer creases. See diagram 15 .

17 This is the location of the previous crease.

18 Make small but neat creases as shown then open the left-hand layer of paper.

19 Make a small crimp as you refold the layers, trapping a tiny triangle of paper in the layers.

Continued next page

Concorde continued

Creative challenge

Using the photograph of the completed model, can you complete the tail section?

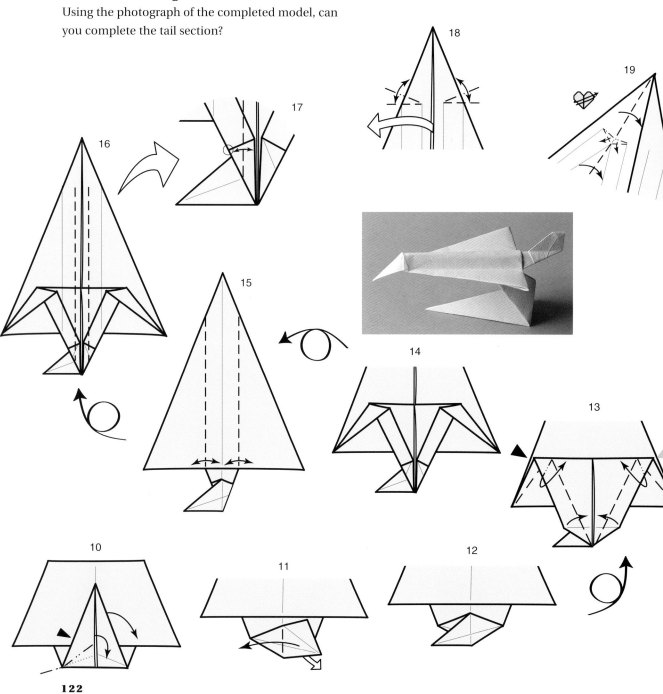

Mushroom

Design by Nick Robinson

This design was created to complement the caterpillar I designed for an Alice in Wonderland origami competition. The caterpillar is now lost for ever (never throw models away unless you have drawn them!), but I diagrammed the mushroom at the time, so it lives on. Shuzo Fujimoto has created a number of boxes and tubes with a flat, twisted end. I noticed that if you alter the angles and proportions, instead of a flat end, you create a conical shape. Once I had "recognized" this as the head of a mushroom, the only remaining design problem was to narrow the stalk. This happens in a rather natural way as you twist the paper. The proportions of the mushroom can be altered at the creasing stage, as explained below.

1. Start with a sheet of A4, or similar rectangle, creased in half both ways. The side nearest to you will become the colored cap of the mushroom. Add vertical one-sixth creases. This produces the "standard" mushroom. If you move the horizontal crease upward (increasing distance "a"), the cap of the mushroom becomes shallower.

2. Turn the paper over and fold the top edge to the horizontal crease.

3. Fold the lower edge to the upper (folded) edge. Open out the double layer.

4. Fold each of the one-sixth sections in half, adding one-twelfth creases where shown. If

Continued next page

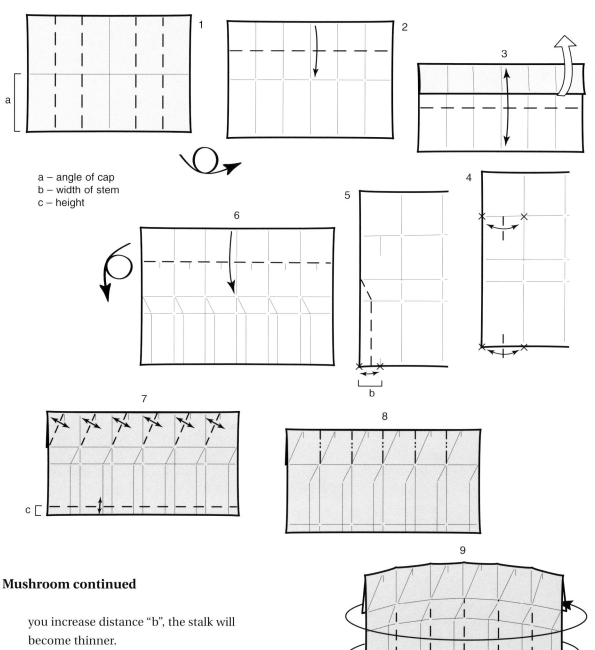

a – angle of cap
b – width of stem
c – height

Mushroom continued

you increase distance "b", the stalk will become thinner.

5 Bisect the left-hand side of each one-twelfth, extending the crease up to the first horizontal crease. At that point, add a crease to meet the next intersection of crease, upward and left.

6 Repeat step 5 on the other five sections. Fold down the top edge on an existing crease.

7 Turn the paper over. Make (sharp) valley creases between the two reference points shown on all six sections. Fold up a small

section at the bottom. The distance "c" determines the height of the mushroom; increasing the distance makes the mushroom shorter.

8 Fold through both layers, making the creases into (sharp) mountain creases.

9   Form the paper into a tube, tucking one end inside the double layers of the other. The six sections reduce to form a five-sided tube.

10 This is the fun part. Using the creases shown, the aim is to collapse the top section into a cone with each internal corner wrapping around the next. This cannot be done a little at a time, but must happen almost as a single movement. My advice is to fold each section into place, to "teach" the paper where it should go, then start all five sections before twisting the paper as a whole and tightening from the inside (use your longest finger!) as well as the outside. Make sure you start with the raw edge (where the paper tucked is into itself) and hold that tightly in place.

11 This is the completed internal arrangement. Well done!

12 Start putting the (existing) creases shown into place, gently twisting the stem as you go.

13 Once the creases are in place, twist further and press the stem up inside the hood.

14 This is the result. The creases should be smooth and the base of the stem as rounded as possible.

15 Lock the base into position by folding in along the existing crease.

16 The completed model.

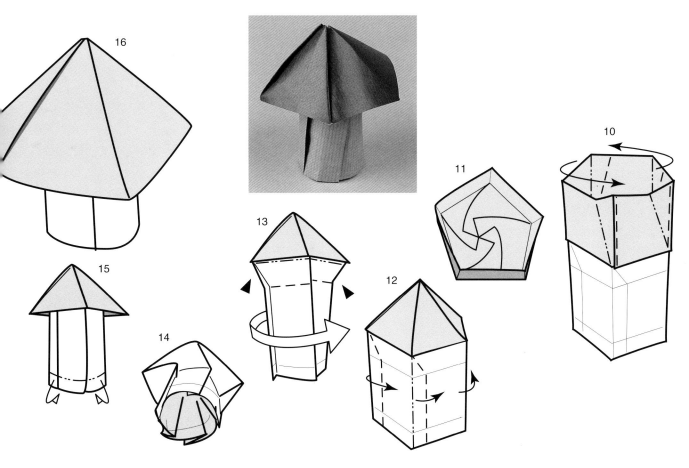

Green Man

Design by Nick Robinson

I have a fascination with origami masks and faces. They are usually simple and expressive, but this one veers toward the more complex end of my work. It is a representation of the "Green Man," a mythical spirit said to inhabit the woods in England during the Middle Ages. It incorporates a technique for creating points devised by the Australian, Steven Casey. The development of the design began with my discovery of a technique for making a nose. I already had a method of forming the mouth, but I needed eyes, too. Making a small square that could be opened into eyes left a series of pleats at the top of the head. I realized that these could also be formed into small squares and could be shaped by folding tiny versions of the familiar Flapping Bird to create stylized hair.

This model will require a large sheet of paper for your first efforts. The paper should also be strong, at least until you have mastered the technique for forming the hair. Be prepared to get halfway and have to start again with a fresh sheet of paper, because the paper can become very "tired" and prone to tearing.

Once you are familiar with the folding method, you might like to take the model to near-completion using paper suitable for wet folding (see the chapter on wet folding). At step 26, wet the paper and shape the face. This will allow you to be more expressive with the molding and shaping.

1   Start with a square, colored side upward. Add one-sixth creases.

2   Add one-twelfth creases with the exception of the bottom one-sixth. Create the same creases at 90 degrees to the originals.

3   Add short valley creases where shown. Note the positions carefully!

4   Turn the paper over and add further, similar, creases.

5   Turn the paper over once more and add the creases that will form the nose. Note that the orientation of the paper is the same as in step 4.

6   Turn the paper over and add further "nose" creases.

7   Fold carefully, using the creases shown and collapse the paper (see diagram 8 for guidance).

8   This shows step 7 from underneath. See diagram 9 to see the finished move. Turn the paper to whichever side makes most sense to you (step 7, this step, or both!) and slowly work toward the finished position.

9   This is the result you are aiming for. Make sure the creases are firmly in place then open the paper out again. Sorry, but it's necessary.

10 Make a series of pleats in the paper.

11 Make similar pleats at 90 degrees.

12 Open the paper out around the top 2 x 2 section. It doesn't matter what happens to the rest of the pleats at this stage, but don't open them out fully.

13 Make sure all your creases match the diagram.

Continued next page

Green Man continued

14 As you collapse the paper on the creases indicated, the central section opens outward to form a type of Preliminary base. Try to fold gently and carefully, or the paper may tear.

15 Make similar folds on the points marked X.

16 Fold the raw edges behind each of the sections, flattening the layer underneath. Check diagram 17 for guidance.

17 The central section resembles an upside-down kite. Fold the lower sides of the kite to the center.

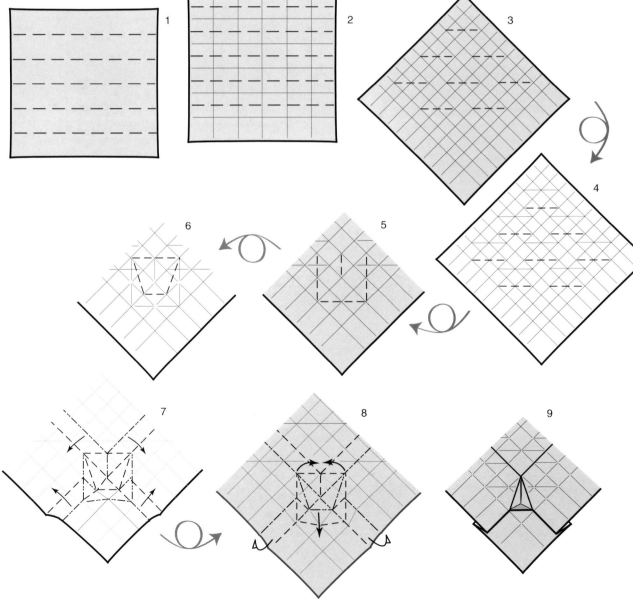

18 Lift the small central flap and swing it upward to form a petal fold.

19 Repeat steps 17 and 18 on the five flaps indicated. Do not fold the two lower points, which will be used to form the eyes.

20 This is the fun part! Re-form the nose section by opening sufficient layers of paper to allow

you access. The two "eye" flaps should be folded halfway out. Take care at the point where the top of the nose meets the eye flaps to keep it as neat as possible.

21 It gets easier now. Make a pleat to form the mouth.

22 Fold the lower sides of the face behind using

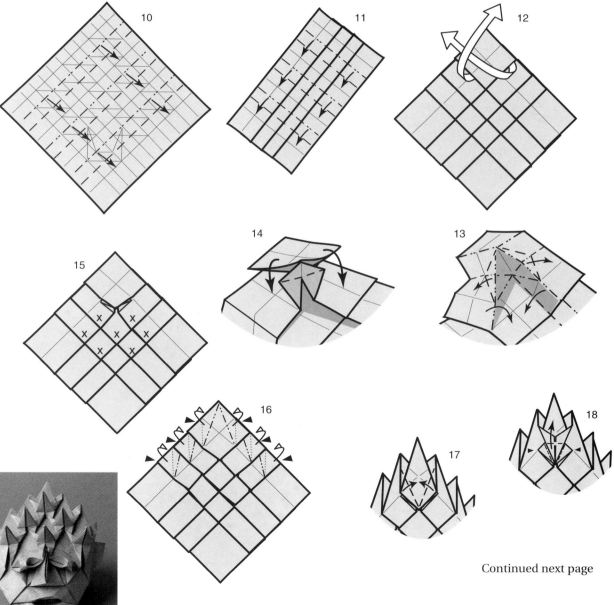

Continued next page

Green Man continued

the mountain creases indicated and squashing a flap behind. Check diagram 23 for guidance.

23 This is the result, seen from underneath. Repeat on the other side.

24 Make a simple pleat to form the ears.

25 To form the eyes, hold the upper layers of the Waterbomb base section and ease them

upward, allowing the center of the paper to squash asymmetrically. This is easier than it sounds. Fold with feeling!

26 Looking from beneath the design, gently round the sides toward you (see the profile). As you do this, fold down the center of the mouth flap. Fold with feeling.

27 You can now open and shape the mouth as you wish. Each time, the result will be subtly

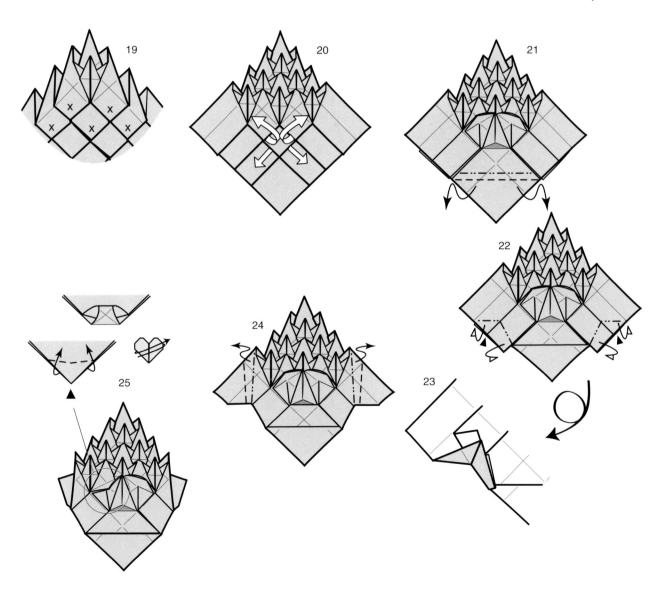

different and will add character to the face.

28 The completed mouth and, indeed, the completed design. Well done!

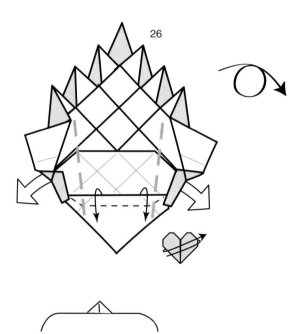

The sides of the face should curve gently towards the rear as in the above top view.

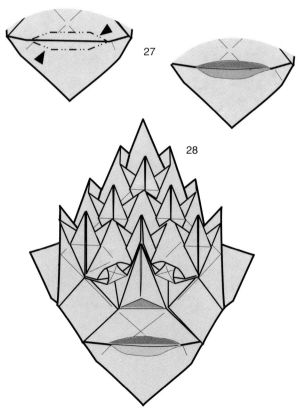

Skeletal Dodecahedron

Design by Robert Neale

The American Robert Neale has devised many classic designs and is recognized worldwide as a creator of great ingenuity and vision. He was among the first to develop a "skeletal" polyhedron – one with "holes" in each of its faces. The unit for this design is perfection in modular origami; it is simple, yet locks together very effectively and has the perfect geometry to create a dodecahedron.

1   Start with a square, colored side upward. Fold in half.

2   Fold a single raw edge back down to the opposite side.

3   Repeat with the remaining raw edge.

4   Fold the lower left corner to meet the top edge. Fold the top right corner to meet the lower edge. Both creases go through all layers. Unfold.

5   Make a crease that joins the inside ends of the creases made in step 4. I find this easier if I turn the paper over and pinch the crease, as in a mountain fold, but it depends on the size of the paper.

6   The unit is now complete. Make a total of 30. Join two together by slipping one corner in between the layers of the next until the two creases overlap. It doesn't matter which pocket the corners go into – one side has one pocket, the other has two.

7   Form a finished corner by slotting a third unit into the first, and tucking the second corner into the third flap. Adjust all three units until the creases coincide.

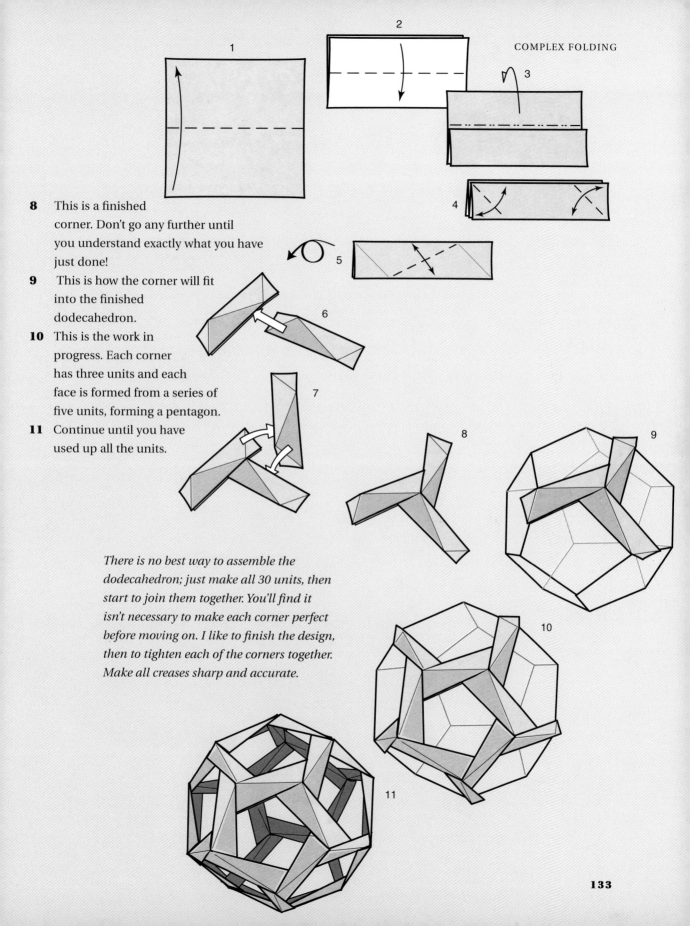

8 This is a finished corner. Don't go any further until you understand exactly what you have just done!

9 This is how the corner will fit into the finished dodecahedron.

10 This is the work in progress. Each corner has three units and each face is formed from a series of five units, forming a pentagon.

11 Continue until you have used up all the units.

There is no best way to assemble the dodecahedron; just make all 30 units, then start to join them together. You'll find it isn't necessary to make each corner perfect before moving on. I like to finish the design, then to tighten each of the corners together. Make all creases sharp and accurate.

Gallery

IT IS BEST TO STUDY origami masterpieces first hand, so you can move around them and see the entire model, and you'll need to contact other folders to do that. In the meantime, here are some designs for you to admire. They reflect a wide range of origami styles and tastes, each according to the designers personal vision of what makes for good origami. As you can see, some folders prefer foil, some use hard creases, others prefer soft creases. Some make large abstract models, others tiny but realistic.

I hope you will draw inspiration from these photographs and use them to suggest new ways in which you can interpret origami designs. Always strive to fold the perfect example and *work with* the paper rather than forcing it into shape. Connoisseurs of origami can always tell when a folder has a good "touch." Once you have mastered a folding sequence, you can then think about things like finesse and choosing a sympathetic type of paper.

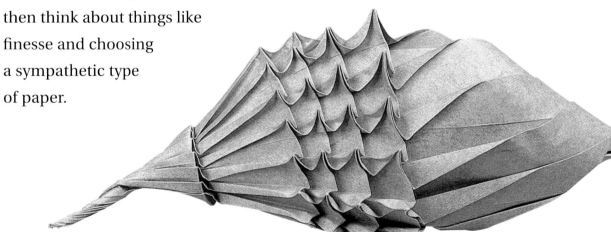

Shell

David Derudas of Italy has an extraordinary communication with the paper. His folding is precise, yet sensitive.

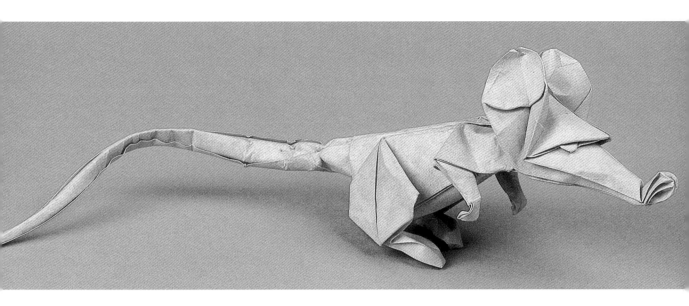

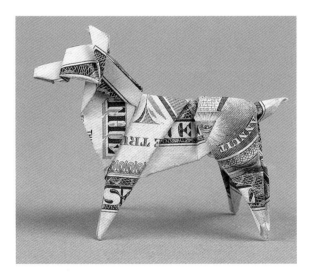

Mouse (ABOVE)

Eric Joisel of France brings a sense of humor and animation to his work. this mouse has a cartoon-like quality, rare in origami.

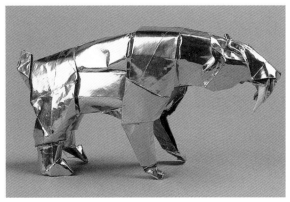

Dollar Dog (ABOVE)

This design of Nick Robinson's brings a number of origami techniques to bear on a dollar bill.

Saber Tooth (ABOVE)

This prehistoric smilodon was created by Satoshi Kamiya, a young Japanese folder of immense talent. It has been beautifully folded by John McKeever.

Floderer (BELOW)

This extraordinary design by Vincent Floderer combines traditional origami bases with an extreme crumpling of the paper to form revolutionary new types of origami.

T Rex (ABOVE)

This T Rex by the author demonstrates that creases don't have to be hard – they can also be soft, adding curves to the model.

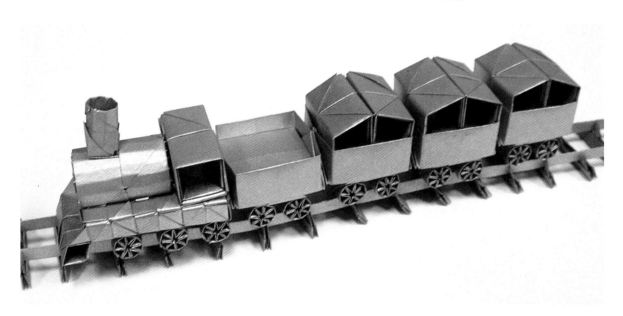

Train (ABOVE)

Toshikazu Kawasaki designed this amazing train, folded by David King from 543 sheets of paper!

Ball (OPPOSITE)

An example of "knotologie" – German Heinz Strobl's name and passion for folding immensely long strips of tape.

Boar (RIGHT)

Another design by Satoshi Kamiya, this "boar god" was also folded by John McKeever.

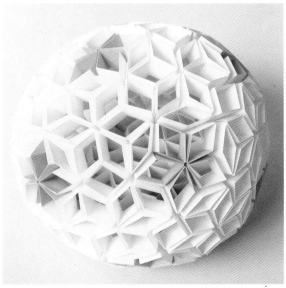

Hand (RIGHT)

This relatively simple design by Tung Ken Lam has been given life and animation by folder Mark Leonard.

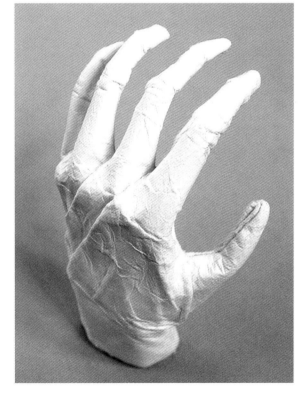

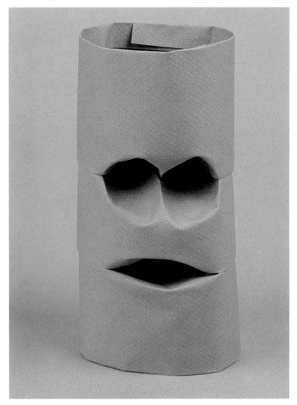

Frog (ABOVE)

American paper artist Michael La Fosse designed and folded this beautiful creature. He even made the sheet of paper with which to fold it.

Mask (RIGHT)

A design by Nick Robinson, exploring a technique called wet-folding, which allows for curved creases to be made.

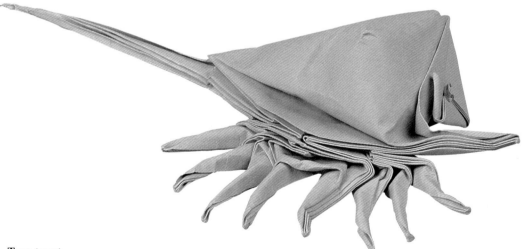

Tree (LEFT)

Impossible though it sounds, this tree has been made from a single sheet of paper by Frenchman Vincent Floderer, using some unique crumpling techniques he has developed.

Shell (ABOVE)

Robert Lang of America designed and folded this shell, part of a fascinating series he has made.

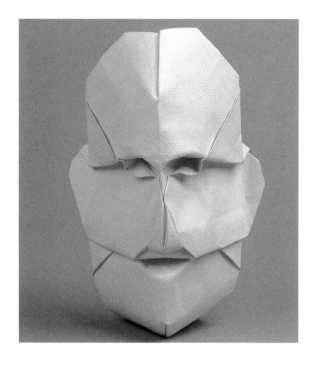

Mask (LEFT)

Another mask from Nick Robinson, who has explored the human face for many years through the medium of paper.

Free Form (BELOW)

A free form creation from Nick Robinson.

Rocket (ABOVE)

Stephenson's rocket is designed by Max Hulme and exquisitely folded by David King. The entire model is no more than 2 inches (5 cms) long.

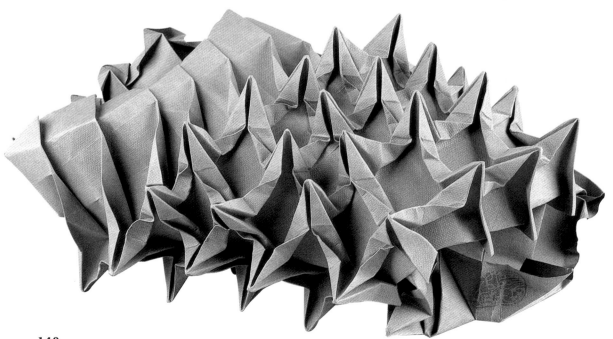

Resources

When you've folded most or even all of the designs in this book, you'll probably be bitten by the origami bug. So what should you do next? Try your local library, who often have several origami books in stock. Fold everything you can get, scour the internet for diagrams, try to find other people nearby who might enjoy folding.

If you're at all serious about origami, you should join an Origami Society. It doesn't even have to be a local one – some people join several! I have been a member of the British Origami Society for the last twenty years and through it have met paper-folders from every corner of the world. Almost without exception, they have been unfailingly polite, unselfish and happy to share their skills and knowledge with no thought of cost. Unlike many activities, origami has never really crossed over into the commercial world and it's still rare to find many paper folders in any one town. For me, this is a bonus, since I feel part of a small but close family.

There are societies all around the world, many with exciting magazines you can subscribe to. From these, you'll never be short of new ideas and things to fold. Many also hold regular conventions where folders from around the world gather to spend a long weekend immersed in paper folding.

As well as thousands of origami diagrams, you can find details of the BOS and other origami societies on the internet. Here are some good places to start.

www.britishorigami.org.uk
www.origami.vancouver.bc.ca
www.12testing.co.uk
(cheesypeas – the author's website)
www.origami-usa.org

You can also write to the BOS membership secretary at
2a the Chestnuts, Countesthorpe, Leicester,
LE8 5TL, England

Index

Biography

Nick Robinson has been folding paper since the early 1980s and has been a member of the British Origami Society for 20 years. He has served on their council for over 10 years. He currently edits their bi-monthly magazine and maintains their website.

Nick spent four years as a professional origami teacher, travelling round schools, libraries, youth clubs, hospitals and art galleries, teaching origami and paper artwork. He ran sessions with people of all ages and physical abilities. His students included both visually and hearing impaired. The arrival of two children obliged him to seek more conventional employment as an IT lecturer, web designer, and author.

He has appeared frequently on television in Britain and Germany, and has fulfilled numerous commissions for magazine, television and Internet advertising campaigns. Over 100 of his original origami creations have been published in 13 countries around the world, including a Japanese newspaper. He has submitted work to many prestigious exhibitions around the world. In 1994 he won three of the five categories for the International Alice in Wonderland Origami competition.

He has written and illustrated over a dozen origami books, with total worldwide sales approaching half a million. Nick lives in Sheffield, England, with wife Alison; children Daisy and Nick; cats Gomez and Matilda, plus geckos Big Dave and Bob. As a former professional musician, he still performs live, mostly solo improvized ambient guitar.

Acknowledgments

I would like to thank the following: Alison, Daisy, Nick, Morticia, and Gomez Robinson for their understanding and whole-hearted support when I was "off on that computer again." If it wasn't for them, the mortgage and the car, I wouldn't have the incentive to write masterpieces like this. My origami friends are too numerous to mention, but David Lister, Dave Brill, Paulo Mulatinho, Edwin Corrie, Kuni Kasahara, Mark Robinson (proof-reader extraordinaire), Francis Ow, Bob Neale, Philip Shen, Mark Kennedy, Gay Gross, and the Hazel Grove mini-meeting crew have all contributed in some way to this book, whether they realize it or not! Also thanks to everyone at Collins & Brown for their work on the project. I must also mention the strangebrews – Mick, John and Joe, plus David Mead and David Torn – for providing the soundtrack to this book. Other vital ingredients included paper by Canson, love hearts by Swizzels, curries by Shaan of London Road. Anyone I've forgotten, please forgive me! Finally, I'd like to dedicate the first proper collection of my work to my late father, who put up with the teenage years, but never had the chance to come for a pint with me.